ARIES

MARCH 21–APRIL 20

2007

J

JOVE BOOKS, NEW YORK

THE BERKLEY PUBLISHING GROUP
Published by the Penguin Group
Penguin Group (USA) Inc.
375 Hudson Street, New York, New York 10014, USA
Penguin Group (Canada), 90 Eglinton Avenue East, Suite 700, Toronto, Ontario M4P 2Y3, Canada
(a division of Pearson Penguin Canada Inc.)
Penguin Books Ltd., 80 Strand, London WC2R 0RL, England
Penguin Group Ireland, 25 St. Stephen's Green, Dublin 2, Ireland (a division of Penguin Books Ltd.)
Penguin Group (Australia), 250 Camberwell Road, Camberwell, Victoria 3124, Australia
(a division of Pearson Australia Group Pty. Ltd.)
Penguin Books India Pvt. Ltd., 11 Community Centre, Panchsheel Park, New Delhi—110 017, India
Penguin Group (NZ), Cnr. Airborne and Rosedale Roads, Albany, Auckland 1310, New Zealand
(a division of Pearson New Zealand Ltd.)
Penguin Books (South Africa) (Pty.) Ltd., 24 Sturdee Avenue, Rosebank, Johannesburg 2196,
South Africa

Penguin Books Ltd., Registered Offices: 80 Strand, London WC2R 0RL, England

The publishers regret that they cannot answer individual letters
requesting personal horoscope information.

2007 TOTAL HOROSCOPE: ARIES

PRINTING HISTORY
Jove edition / June 2006

ISBN: 0-515-14103-8

JOVE®
Jove Books are published by The Berkley Publishing Group,
a division of Penguin Group (USA) Inc.,
375 Hudson Street, New York, New York 10014.
Jove and the "J" design are registered trademarks of Penguin Group (USA) Inc.

PRINTED IN THE UNITED STATES OF AMERICA

10 9 8 7 6 5 4 3 2 1

CONTENTS

MESSAGE TO ARIES

Dear Aries,

If there's a situation that requires positive action and healthy initiative, plunge right in. Don't worry about whether you should or shouldn't. Just do it and in the doing you will find yourself. Action will give you the courage to act. Initiative will add confidence to your character. Youthful zest will help put plans into swing and your approach will be positive, direct, energetic, and optimistic.

You're a strong-willed human being deep down and at your best you stand up for what you believe in—yourself. No matter how you may shrink from danger or confrontation you can be tough and fiery. You *can* be bold and daring and do whatever you must to attain your ends. You have strong impulses to do exactly as you please, take chances, try something new, get into new ventures, and be off on your own; yet external commitments often pose problems you just can't simply wipe out. You still have to deal with people.

You can't take life easy for too long. You're a positive, productive person when you can take healthy decisive action. But for that you need confidence. Without confidence you can be brash, crude, and hostile, and come on with a harsh air of noisy bravado that can turn people off.

To get the confidence you need, learn to recognize an opportunity and act on it. In this sense be practical. If you move too soon or too late you can spoil the timing. Develop your nose and learn to sniff out what's good for you. Move in when you can and then don't wreck your own chances.

You fear action because you either do not feel good about yourself or you jump in first and notice the crocodiles afterward. So you can flounder because of the holes in your own ego, or meet countless other crises through a thoughtless, impulsive manner. In a way, you are naive and immature, but that gives you a stubbornly youthful capacity for renewal. You can patch things up and start over, so even your serious blunders can be taken in stride.

Sitting around and waiting for miracles is unwholesome for you. You should be an active creator of your own fortune; a passive mystical approach to life has only limited value for you. Any mystical connection with the infinite is found in dynamism. Thus, your life is rarely easy because you need to build universes and make worlds. You are bored quickly and always need to cut through jungles and carve your way to a new life. You don't like to wait for the laggards at the back of the line and you despise yourself when you are trailing behind. You have the ambition to be a leader, but are often an unpopular one. If you are ever to get voted number one, you need to cultivate your sense of the other person. Confidence plus cooperation brings success with people.

Your vibrancy and competitive urge for immediate results can spur you on to action, action, and more action. Completing what you start isn't always important to you (though you may think and say it is), since you constantly crave newness and challenge. Your nose is at the front of civilization. You're at the head of the wagon train. You're perceptive, quick-witted, intelligent, inventive, creative, and gifted. As a human being you are noble and inspiring, fighting for the underdog in an unending battle for human rights. Often you are more involved with the fight for peace than the peace itself. You have many ideas with fresh approaches to many problems. Try to increase your natural decisiveness and clear a path for leadership and iniative.

Don't ever let conflicts or crises get you down. Learn to balance your arguments. When you are convinced you're right you refuse to listen to others. You detest domination or restrictions. You loathe having your impulses curtailed.

There are days when you feel dashingly beautiful, innocently happy, brave, inspired, helpful, loving, and deserving of all that is wonderful. Then there are days when you are cranky and hostile. You can be pushy and act tougher than you are. You may be conceited and obnoxious, selfish and cruel, and whack everyone down while speaking up for your own ends in the name of righteousness. Frank and candid when it suits you, you repress these traits in others. Up one minute, down the next. Yet through it all you pop up with an invincibility that is both exasperating and inspiring to others.

Leaving things unfinished is not always a solution, since you invariably run into the same problems over and over until they're completely worked out. Uniting your unbridled drive with method and responsibility is another way of improving your confidence and self-image. Obstacles can stimulate you and provide you with the sensitivity you need to conquer and win, which are your chief goals though you often deny it.

It's not always a question of being brave enough to take the plunge. Sometimes it's more an issue of learning to get in step with rhythms and cycles which are not entirely in your control. Maybe it's ultimately not your responsibility to take care of all the loose ends. Maybe when you get the urge to move on, or the forces of destiny call you, you simply must go and leave it all behind. You must do what you must do in this life. Although every action causes a reaction you must not fear action because of the possible consequences. Right conduct, even in its most noble form, will often make waves. Don't be afraid of the waves. Our lives are usually deeply wrapped up with those around us. Threads of interaction, webs of human relationships, are so intricately woven that everything we do produces a reaction in the lives of the people around us. But when something must be done in your life, sometimes you just have to do it.

It's not easy for your Aries nature to become diplomatic, for basically you are not. Although you cool off quickly and forgive easily, your angry acts of aggression can cause long-lasting hurt in others. You tend to press and insist just when patience, tact, and understanding are called for. Try not to resent criticism. Use objectivity and patience to develop your projects and relationships with nourishing temperate care. Resilience, self-reliance, and love of life should be combined with cooperation and consideration for others. The desire to be self-governing is an instinct you must never lose. Couple it with your awareness of the needs of other human beings. The outcome of human relationships depends on the blend of ego demands and concessions, self-reliance and diplomacy. Exciting figures come into your life, in addition to dangers, confrontations, and partnerships, all making demands for the transformation of your nature. You must stand up and face the challenge, see yourself more clearly than ever for what you really are, and define what matters most to you. Minimize the weaknesses and maximize the strengths. Your greatest enemy is inaction. Activity is your source of renewal.

You are truly an energetic person with many ideas, ambitions, and talents. When things start to bore, you tend to drop them. So direct yourself to an area where you will be constantly pitting yourself against new situations and challenges, new projects and problems. You'll be happiest when you have a strong measure of control over your own life. That will make you feel successful. You can be a warm, charming companion, and you add a streak of something alive and openly masterful to anyone's life. You can cajole, persuade, and argue, convince, win over, and seduce. You do have a strong capacity for decisive behavior in a crisis, and this is an asset in developing either salesmanship or artistry. You have the drive to win of a military general, but you often lack skill with people. Although you could really be weak in bedside manner despite your genuine feeling, you would still make a splendid doctor or professional person. You're often at home in any kind of business where aggressive behavior is most readily accepted.

Your bright, outgoing manner still attracts people. When you're not feeling argumentative or pugnacious, you have a winning way. You can defeat your opposition with a smile and go on without losing a moment. People like you and making friends is easy. Friendship can be fast and furious while it's new, but can soon exhaust itself and collapse, often through clashes and conflicts of interest. Your enthusiasm and quick shift of interest will frequently extend to people as well as work projects and ideas, for it is usually the newness you find fascinating and absorbing.

You probably feel you're not independent enough on some level, professional or personal. You are devoted to figuring out ways to assert yourself on one level or another. You want to be strong, positive, and aggressive, heading toward your first or your millionth love affair. You strive to be outgoing and friendly and often bury, quite successfully, any insecurities you may have beneath the bravado of a busy, independent life. When you're turned on, you are active, bold, and dynamic, often attracting a shy, dependent type. You face hardship and trouble with a courageous approach, willing everything to come out all right. You believe you are what you make of yourself and you want to hold destiny in your own hands. You prefer to live in candid idealism, wrestling with the devil himself if need be, and winning, of course. You live on because of your fantastic life resource: resilience.

Yours can be the story of success and renewal, different versions of the hero winning at everything: the rock star's first smash hit, the challenger becoming the champ, explorers discovering worlds. You are unimpeachably and creatively your own person. You are not your mother. You are not your father. You are you! And because you are so undeniably, uncontrollably, irrepressibly you, there is no pattern you have to repeat, nobody's rule you just have to follow. You possess a magic button that releases fuel, fire, and enough energy to light a thousand cities. Sexually, you are a potential dynamo. Each moment of your life is as new and magnificent as a sunrise, for you reflect the creative potential of a new day. You have your bad moments, of course: brief, dark depressions that are like quick blackouts against the backdrop of a long continuous stream of light. But ultimately you are bright and positive. Vote for yourself and take yourself for what you are. Don't dwell on limitations or ponder problems too seriously.

Some Aries are anything but aggressive and everything but independent. You are shy and introspective, with very little confidence. You think about doing more often than you do, and when you finally make a move you doubt all your actions and judgment. You are kind and thoughtful (which you don't mind admitting), gentle, considerate, helpful, and tender, putting yourself everywhere but first. You may be an Aries who is a quiet, timid, peaceful sort of person who doesn't really enjoy being on your own.

If you lack courage, confidence, and self-esteem, you have a problem to unravel. You may have to temper your self-oriented boldness with your respect for other human beings and channel your ego into useful or realistic action. You may thus be unable to allow yourself the freedom you think you deserve. You may be fighting an inward struggle with a desire to be free of all encumbrances, to eradicate or to destroy the very roots of your being. Whether you've been indifferent or indolent, inconsistent or fearful, now is the time to work consistently and systematically to build a new self-image. You can then fulfill your ambitions and force yourself to new heights of success.

In order to do this, you have to deal with the limitations that hamper you. Impatient with old conditions, social status, and personal restrictions, your resistance and rebelliousness point toward a whole new course of action. You must first make the transformation on a mental plane before you can change your everyday existence. You must think through the meaning of liberation, if it means freedom to break old ties, get away from family and friends, change personality, be someone else, or try something entirely new. Sexual breakthroughs and intellectual challenges are all part of the process of liberation. Whatever your choice of change, it must be the right one in order for you to lead a happy and satisfying life.

If you're in a personal relationship, don't bother to try to figure out who is the stronger one. It's often virtually impossible to tell. Sometimes the more outwardly bold and aggressive member of the pair is really the more dependent, deep down. If you are shy or unable to act out your feelings or urges, you need to find a direct way to rebuild your feeling of self-worth. Otherwise, you may act in unhealthy, ignoble ways or even turn the hostility inward upon yourself through physical weakness or disease. You cannot really let yourself be totally ruled or dominated by others. At some point you have to answer to yourself. It is often said that without a healthy self-image, it is hard to accomplish anything in this life, and that situation may be your special paradox.

Your desire for self-rule may be in conflict with a subtle lack of motivation or an inability to cooperate or work steadily and consistently toward the completion of tasks. Sometimes your reluctance to face the more complex sides of your personality is the very thing that holds you back. True, you're not very analytical as a rule, so your greatest successes depend more on your instantaneous response to challenge and crisis than your hashing over the past. What's done is done. Now you have to go on from here. But if you are not to go repeating mistake after mistake, you may need to grasp whatever it is that is eating at you, face it, and conquer it once and for all.

Whatever your paradox, the basic issue is the supremacy of the human will over all obstacles, limitations, threats, catastrophes, or conflicts. Aries represents the success of individuality over everything. Symbolized by the sunrise of a new day, it's a life not always based on facts, reason, or a realistic approach. It is the magic hunch, the action that brings amazing results. Of course, thoughtless impetuosity can cut a path of wide destruction, bitterness, and regret. The battle for ego supremacy can finish with a Pyrrhic victory where there is no real winner.

Yet is it impossible for one person to tell anyone else when it's time to move or act, declare war, or stand up for beliefs. That's the point of Aries: knowing when to seize an opportunity, take initiative and responsibility, and do something. The consciousness of action is generated from within and can most assuredly be cultivated and developed.

Your gift to the Zodiac is the spark of life that wipes away the past. It is rebirth of light out of the darkness, the beginning, creation, springtime. You must maintain that inextinguishable force of life, light, enthusiasm, and strength that comes from the energy of just being yourself, for better or worse, like it or not.

Michael Lutin

ARIES SNEAK PREVIEW OF THE 21st CENTURY

As the decade opens on a new century, indeed on a new millennium, the planets set the stage for change and challenge. Themes connecting present and future are in play. Already, planetary influences that emerged from the century just past are showing the drama unfolding in the twenty-first century. These influences reveal hidden paths and personal hints for achieving your potential—your message from the planets.

Aries individuals, ruled by fiery Mars, will be guided by the interplay between Jupiter, the good-luck planet, and Saturn, the taskmaster planet. Aries should also look to Pluto, planet of beginnings and endings.

The great power of Pluto in Sagittarius, another fire sign, may already be starting its transformation of your character and lifestyle. Pluto in Sagittarius from late 1995 into the year 2008 creates a significant change in your idea pattern. As you move around more, the way you make a living may be fluctuating. As you explore through travel or education, your economic and material resources will be shifting. The strong idealistic aspects that Pluto in Sagittarius makes with your own Sun sign can give plenty of inspiration to fire your Aries imagination.

Because of the influences of Jupiter and Saturn, communications will be emphasized, especially toward the middle of the decade from 2003 through 2006. With Jupiter in Leo, Virgo, Libra, and Scorpio during these years, work in the media can be lively and lucrative. Aries on stage, on screen, in the public eye in any way can use expressive talents to make the world a better place. Saturn in Gemini and in Cancer provides depth and inspiration to writing and thought. Saturn in Leo from 2005 to 2007 hones performance and creative skills. Saturn also poses issues of long-term security versus immediate gratification. For a second chance to make good in love and in money, look to Jupiter and to Saturn.

Significant in 2004, 2005, and 2006 is a solar eclipse and New Moon taking place in your sign of Aries. Such a planetary event, especially in 2006, can be a strong signal of new beginnings, of change, for some of you. How others perceive you can be important. You may be impelled to transform your image, your views, even your lifestyle.

But as you attempt to change things, there can be conflicts between love and money, or money and work. There also is a danger of spreading yourself too thin, of starting and stopping, of abandoning a project before it has come to fruition. Significant crises can be turned into great successes or dismal failures depending on how you approach your goals. Finally, there is a possibility that, if you lose your idealism, ambition becomes narrow and self-centered, thinking becomes smug and traditional.

Never turn your back on the mysteries of life. Uranus and Neptune, both planets of enlightenment and renewed idealism, give you glimpses into the future, let you peek through the secret doorway. With Uranus in Pisces from March 2003 to May 2010, a strongly intuitive force urges work and service for the good of humankind. You can be in the forefront of change, your efforts can accelerate social reform. Neptune in Aquarius 1998 into the year 2012 gives full flower to your curiosity, your urge to explore and create, and your vision to help the people around you. A reminder to Aries in the new century: as you seize responsibility, remember to share the glory.

THE CUSP-BORN ARIES

Are you *really* an Aries? If your birthday falls during the fourth week of March, at the beginning of Aries, will you still retain the traits of Pisces, the sign of the Zodiac before Aries? What if you were born late in April—are you more Taurus than Aries? Many people born at the edge, or cusp, of a sign have difficulty determining exactly what sign they are. If you are one of these people, here's how you can figure it out, once and for all.

Consult the table on page 17. Find the year of your birth, and then note the day. The table will tell you the precise days on which the Sun entered and left your sign for the year of your birth. If you were born at the beginning or end of Aries, yours is a lifetime reflecting a process of subtle transformation. Your life on Earth will symbolize a significant change in consciousness, for you are either about to enter a whole new way of living or are leaving one behind.

If your birthday falls at the end of March, you may want to read the horoscope book for Pisces as well as Aries, for Pisces holds the keys to many of your hidden uncertainties, past guilts, weaknesses, sorrows, unspoken wishes, and your cosmic unfoldment.

You are eager to start living, and possess, in a way, the secret of eternal youth. Obstacles enrage you but never beat you, for you usually feel you have sacrificed more than your share. In some way (after waiting) you will assert yourself and your right to make your own decisions.

However, though, you are often drawn back through

Pisces into a sense of responsibility, a duty to others, and a selfishness that at times eats away at your confidence and undermines your character. Honor and the vitality of life are your gifts.

If you were born late in April, you may want to read the horoscope book for Taurus as well as Aries. The investment could be revealing and profitable, for Taurus is often your means of putting your talents to practical use and turning your ideas into tangible rewards.

You are headstrong and determined; you have a sense of independence and fight that nothing can destroy. Sometimes you can vacillate and be worried and negative, but you never give up. You have the earthy sense of all your needs to meet responsibilities, do your duties, build, acquire, and collect. You are attracted to all you possess, and the more you possess, the more permanent your life. You are thus less able to simply pick up and go back to zero; what you start you must try to finish.

THE CUSPS OF ARIES

DATES SUN ENTERS ARIES
(LEAVES PISCES)

March 20 every year from 1900 to 2010,
except for the following:

March 21

1901	1911	1923	1938	1955
02	13	26	39	59
03	14	27	42	63
05	15	30	43	67
06	18	31	46	71
07	19	34	47	75
09	22	35	51	79
10				

DATES SUN LEAVES ARIES
(ENTERS TAURUS)

April 20 every year from 1900 to 2010,
except for the following:

April 19				April 21
1948	1972	1988	2000	1903
52	76	89	2001	07
56	80	92	2004	11
60	81	93	2005	19
64	84	96	2008	
68	85	97	2009	

ARIES RISING:
YOUR ASCENDANT

Could you be a "double" Aries? That is, could you have Aries as your Rising sign as well as your Sun sign? The tables on pages 20–21 will tell you Aries what your Rising sign happens to be. Just find the hour of your birth, then find the day of your birth, and you will see which sign of the Zodiac is your Ascendant, as the Rising sign is called. For a detailed discussion on how the Rising sign is determined, see pages 82–85.

Your Ascendant, or Rising sign, modifies your basic Sun sign personality, and it affects the way you act out the daily predictions for your Sun sign. If your Rising sign is indeed Aries, what follows is a description of its effects on your horoscope. If your Rising sign is some other sign of the Zodiac, you may wish to read the horoscope book for that sign as well.

With Aries Rising, look to planet Mars, the ruler of Aries. Mars gives you undaunted courage and strong recuperative powers. It makes you extraordinarily resistant to stress, strain, and sickness. You are especially lucky in that you probably will live a long life bent on success. The planet Pluto is often regarded as co-ruler of Aries. Pluto together with Mars can increase your chances of success. Pluto has a banishing effect on enemies and troubles. Just when you feel most hard pressed by personal loss or public enmity, Pluto negates the power of these harmful forces.

Aries Rising people stamp the environment with vitality. You have a great need for instant success, which imparts an urgency to all your undertakings. You are a picture of boundless energy, unlimited courage, untapped reserves. In love, in work, in study, you want rewards right away. As soon as the need is gratified, you may lose interest. At times you don't stay around to see things through. Some may say you lack foresight, but you do see a brighter horizon elsewhere. Your vision is as bold as your bid for self-actualization.

You are a loner, fiercely guarding your independence. You can be overconfident, sometimes boastful. You thrive on challenge. Reckless of danger, you often invite competition and combat. And you frequently gain by these means. You keenly feel oppression, being aware how rank, responsibility, and privilege confer power. If you cannot be at the head of things, you want at least a free hand. If you feel restricted, you may not participate. These traits make some of you poor team players, others of you notorious rebels.

Those of you with Aries Rising are blessed with the knack of invention. You know how to fix things. A good judge of character and situation, you swiftly size up a scene. You are handy and creative. You are eager to go ahead, to make daring new moves. Sometimes you are overeager, hasty, shortsighted. You scorn defeat, though, so no loss holds you back. Like the Ram, your zodiacal symbol, you butt your way through the obstacles.

Personal fulfillment is a driving force, and some people find you insensitive as you sweep forward. Your anger can be a blunt weapon at times leading to revenge, careless action, disorderly behavior. Combined with righteousness, anger can make you a formidable opponent of antiquated ideas, of a society rigid with restrictions. Aries Rising creates the character of the fearless pioneer.

The key words for Aries Rising are impulse and action. Self-fulfillment comes through a balance of these forces in order to meet the challenges of material success and inner growth.

RISING SIGNS FOR ARIES

Hour of Birth*	Day of Birth		
	March 20–25	March 26–30	March 31–April 4
Midnight	Sagittarius	Sagittarius	Sagittarius
1 AM	Sagittarius	Sagittarius; Capricorn 3/28	Capricorn
2 AM	Capricorn	Capricorn	Capricorn
3 AM	Capricorn	Capricorn; Aquarius 3/27	Aquarius
4 AM	Aquarius	Aquarius	Aquarius; Pisces 4/3
5 AM	Pisces	Pisces	Pisces
6 AM	Pisces; Aries 3/23	Aries	Aries
7 AM	Aries	Aries; Taurus 3/27	Taurus
8 AM	Taurus	Taurus	Taurus; Gemini 4/3
9 AM	Gemini	Gemini	Gemini
10 AM	Gemini	Gemini	Gemini; Cancer 4/2
11 AM	Cancer	Cancer	Cancer
Noon	Cancer	Cancer	Cancer
1 PM	Cancer; Leo 3/23	Leo	Leo
2 PM	Leo	Leo	Leo
3 PM	Leo	Leo	Virgo
4 PM	Virgo	Virgo	Virgo
5 PM	Virgo	Virgo	Virgo
6 PM	Virgo; Libra 3/24	Libra	Libra
7 PM	Libra	Libra	Libra
8 PM	Libra	Libra	Scorpio
9 PM	Scorpio	Scorpio	Scorpio
10 PM	Scorpio	Scorpio	Scorpio
11 PM	Scorpio; Sagittarius 3/22	Sagittarius	Sagittarius

*See footnote on facing page.

Hour of Birth*	Day of Birth		
	April 5–9	April 10–14	April 15–20
Midnight	Sagittarius	Sagittarius; Capricorn 4/12	Capricorn
1 AM	Capricorn	Capricorn	Capricorn
2 AM	Capricorn	Capricorn; Aquarius 4/11	Aquarius
3 AM	Aquarius	Aquarius	Aquarius; Pisces 4/18
4 AM	Pisces	Pisces	Pisces
5 AM	Pisces; Aries 4/7	Aries	Aries
6 AM	Aries	Aries; Taurus 4/11	Taurus
7 AM	Taurus	Taurus	Taurus; Gemini 4/18
8 AM	Gemini	Gemini	Gemini
9 AM	Gemini	Gemini	Gemini; Cancer 4/17
10 AM	Cancer	Cancer	Cancer
11 AM	Cancer	Cancer	Cancer
Noon	Cancer; Leo 4/8	Leo	Leo
1 PM	Leo	Leo	Leo
2 PM	Leo	Leo	Virgo
3 PM	Virgo	Virgo	Virgo
4 PM	Virgo	Virgo	Virgo
5 PM	Virgo; Libra 4/7	Libra	Libra
6 PM	Libra	Libra	Libra
7 PM	Libra	Libra; Scorpio 4/14	Scorpio
8 PM	Scorpio	Scorpio	Scorpio
9 PM	Scorpio	Scorpio	Scorpio
10 PM	Scorpio; Sagittarius 4/1	Sagittarius	Sagittarius
11 pm	Sagittarius	Sagittarius	Sagittarius

*Hour of birth given here is for Standard Time in any time zone. If your hour of birth was recorded in Daylight Saving Time, subtract one hour from it and consult that hour in the table above. For example, if you were born at 6 AM D.S.T., see 5 AM above.

LOVE AND RELATIONSHIPS

No matter who you are, what you do in life, or where your planets are positioned, you still need to be loved, and to feel love for other human beings. Human relationships are founded on many things: infatuation, passion, sex, guilt, friendship, and a variety of other complex motivations, frequently called love.

Relationships often start out full of hope and joy, the participants sure of themselves and sure of each other's love, and then end up more like a pair of gladiators than lovers. When we are disillusioned, bitter, and wounded, we tend to blame the other person for difficulties that were actually present long before we ever met. Without seeing clearly into our own natures we will be quite likely to repeat our mistakes the next time love comes our way.

Enter Astrology.

It is not always easy to accept, but knowledge of ourselves can improve our chances for personal happiness. It is not just by predicting when some loving person will walk into our lives, but by helping us come to grips with our failures and reinforce our successes.

Astrology won't solve all our problems. The escapist will ultimately have to come to terms with the real world around him. The hard-bitten materialist will eventually acknowledge the eternal rhythms of the infinite beyond which he can see or hear. Astrology does not merely explain away emotion. It helps us unify the head with the heart so that we can become whole individuals. It helps us define what it is we are searching for, so we can recognize it when we find it.

Major planetary cycles have been changing people's ideas about love and commitment, marriage, partnerships, and relationships. These cycles have affected virtually everyone in areas of personal involvement. Planetary forces point out upheavals and transformations occurring in all of society. The concept of marriage is being totally reexamined. Exactly what the changes will ultimately bring no one can tell. It is usually difficult to determine which direction society will take. One thing is certain: no man is an island. If the rituals and pomp of wedding ceremonies must be revised, then it will happen.

Social rules are being revised. Old outworn institutions are indeed crumbling. But relationships will not die. People are putting less stress on permanence and false feelings of security. The emphasis now shifts toward the union of two loving souls. Honesty, equality, and mutual cooperation are the goals in modern marriage. When these begin to break down, the marriage is in jeopardy. Surely there must be a balance between selfish separatism and prematurely giving up.

There is no doubt that astrology can establish the degree of compatibility between two human beings. Two people can share a common horizon in life but have quite different habits or basic interests. Two others might have many basic characteristics in common while needing to approach their goals from vastly dissimilar points of view. Astrology describes compatibility based on these assumptions.

It compares and contrasts through the fundamental characteristics that draw two people together. Although they could be at odds on many basic levels, two people could find themselves drawn together again and again. Sometimes it seems that we keep being attracted to the same type of individuals. We might ask ourselves if we have learned anything from our past mistakes. The answer is that there are qualities in people that we require and thus seek out time and time again. To solve that mystery in ourselves is to solve much of the dilemma of love, and so to help ourselves determine if we are approaching a wholesome situation or a potentially destructive one.

We are living in a very curious age with respect to marriage and relationships. We can easily observe the shifting social attitudes concerning the whole institution of marriage. People are seeking everywhere for answers to their own inner needs. In truth, all astrological combinations can achieve compatibility. But many relationships seem doomed before they get off the ground. Astrologically there can be too great a difference between the goals, aspirations, and personal outlook of the people involved. Analysis of both horoscopes must and will indicate enough major planetary factors to keep the two individuals together. Call it what you will: determination, patience, understanding, love—whatever it may be, two people have the capacity to achieve a state of fulfillment together. We all have different needs and desires. When it comes to choosing a mate, you really have to know yourself. If you know the truth about what you are really looking for, it will make it easier to find. Astrology is a useful, almost essential, tool to that end.

In the next chapter your basic compatibility with each of the twelve signs of the Zodiac is generalized. The planetary vibrations between you and an individual born under any given zodiacal sign suggest much about how you will relate to each other. Hints are provided about love and romance, sex and marriage so that you and your mate can get the most out of the relationship that occupies so important a role in your life.

ARIES:
YOU AND YOUR MATE

ARIES—ARIES

This is an exciting contest of wills. Assuming you ever agree on enough of each other's ideas to have any sort of union, yours is a relationship based on motivation and drive. You are a powerful case of like attracting like. You both share the spirit of adventure that flows through every Aries man and woman, and you engender excitement and energy in each other. You can fire each other up with enthusiasm, competition, and challenge, simply by the force and power of your own will.

On an emotional level, this is a mighty powerful collision. These days the key to successful relationships is equality but you'll both have to put up with a lot of jockeying for power, no matter who seems to be the weaker of the two. The battle for supremacy can end up in a total deadlock or in an explosive separation. If you don't grant each other freedom and the right to be, there will be no relationship.

You are both warm, amorous, and ambitious, but you are not the perfect example of the share-and-share-alike couple. You both need something to keep your interest in each other, and without the ingredient of constant stimulation, your mutual attraction could turn into repulsion. You both need outlets for your energy.

Hints for Your Aries Mate

If you treat your Aries partner just the way you would want to be treated, moment for moment, you will not be taken by surprise or disappointed by the reaction. After all, you both are children of the Ram, and the capacity for willfulness in the relationship doubles the norm. Don't jockey for position; alternate the dominating and subordinate roles in your relationship. Support and sacrifice, which both individuals of a couple need at different times, must be a function that each of you fulfills. It won't do to squelch your partner's outside interests. And you must be fair, yet tactful, to preserve your own. Otherwise one or both of you will see the intrusion as a choking of independence. On the other hand, don't let your own interests, or your mate's, foster a hostile competition between you. Rather, let people and activities come into your lives, separately as well as together, so you can keep up the sparkle in your partnership.

ARIES—TAURUS

Idealism meets practicality here. Taurus can be your greatest asset, for the sheer immovable force you will encounter every time you get restless or obnoxious will bring you down to Earth and make you think in simple terms of dollars and cents, and your earthly needs.

Sometimes the very qualities that attracted you to Taurus can be hard to cope with, for you are both growing at different rates and in different ways. What you may look upon as stubborn, unyielding obstinacy can be loyalty, endurance, and constancy—a strong stillness that is highly attractive and exciting. You can undermine Taurus when the chips are down, or you can provide encouragement and strength. Your unceasing energy and command over yourself (believe it or not) are the major components of your allure for Taurus.

It's not easy for Taurus to be pushed into action without careful consideration. As far as you're concerned, when you stand still for too long, you're all through. You are both pleasure lovers, but your orientation to life is usually different. It is speed versus certainty, trial-and-error versus order. This combination will tempt and control each of you in the extreme at the same time.

Hints for Your Taurus Mate

At all times, be friendly with your Taurus mate, whose sweet nature reflects the affection of Venus, their planetary ruler. Don't strive for glamour or heady emotion; that will only confuse Taurus into thinking a crisis is imminent, rather than just your own style of getting close asserting itself. Value your mate's need for comfort and good fun on a steady basis. Supply them without recklessness, and try very hard not to break appointments, be late, or switch plans. Your Taurus mate will be chagrined by challenges to his or her basic passivity, and will punish you by withdrawing. So don't push ideas or ambitions until you have spent a lot of time and discussion on them. Seeds need to be planted, and Taurus likes to germinate them until they are ready for harvest. Plant gently. Play down any dogmatism in your personality, and certainly do not be flippant romantically. Your relationship flowers the best in a deception-free environment.

ARIES—GEMINI

Your relationship is a dynamic one. That is, between you there is the ceaseless interchange of thought and energy, the urge to explore, travel around, experiment, and communicate. It could exhaust itself quickly, like a fast hot flame that burns out soon after ignition. But you are both positive, active creatures deep down, both gifted at bringing new elements, new surroundings, and general versatility into the relationship and thus keeping it vital, fluid, and alive. Sometimes those new elements will be a source of conflict, since each of you will feel threatened when it comes to your partner's tireless need for innovation and experimentation.

But you are pals, after all. Sometimes you can gab like teenage cousins. Such a relationship can have a friendship of a platonic quality that lacks strong emotions or depth on major levels. So from time to time you may both get restless. The frantic, hectic kind of liaison so possible for Aries and Gemini can be a mere puff of smoke, but don't sell it short. Remain friends. This blend can be a source of long-lasting companionship, as long as you part and come back together from time to time to swap stories and share successes.

Hints for Your Gemini Mate

As with any advice geared to a Twin, which your Gemini mate indeed is, there are double messages and they are contradictory. First, do exactly what you did when captivation hooked you both; keep it light and adventurous. Second, be totally different; you're a parent figure now. Go out a lot; nothing dispels gloom from the heart of an anxious Gemini than a treat on the town or a drive to a quaint place. Fun doesn't have to be exotic or expensive—just novel. Stay in a lot and talk; your Gemini mate needs to tell all, so be there to listen and ask questions. Don't force your view of life on your Gemini partner; pretend that your insights are spontaneous and gratuitous and that he or she need not accept them. Be a steadying influence; guide your Gemini mate into meaningful pursuits and out of foolish ones. Don't be a boss; share the responsibilities of your partnership. Be a manager; make decisions subtly so your Gemini feels liberated and at the same time the liberator.

ARIES—CANCER

If your relationship has survived the almost unbelievable amount of disruption and interference of the last decade, you can thank your own positive response to challenge and your Cancer's patient staying power.

Many marriages will not have survived these forces, since they have been subjected to bombardment from unexpected reversals and social changes and the revision of all views on marriage and security, and on the way people behave in family situations. It's a question of personal independence, really.

If you have made it through together, you're both very changed. You can still get angry at the drop of a hat, and Cancer can still crawl under cover instantaneously. But now your better view of yourselves and each other will make you aware of the growing transformation taking place.

Changes that are slow in coming are usually the longest lasting. The success of your relationship depends on your appreciation of each other's integrity. Your Aries power of expansion and desire for new encounters will always be in conflict with Cancer's sense of family responsibility. That's healthy.

Hints for Your Cancer Mate

If you are in a long-standing relationship with a Moon Child, as your Cancer mate is affectionately called, you still may not truly know him or her, who is very hard to know. Honor that protective shell, which after all is your mate's defense against being hurt or unfairly influenced. That very same structure will be put to your service when you feel hedged and hounded by life's creditors; your Cancer mate can be a formidable ally on your behalf. So don't expose your mate to critiques of the psychological kind, and do not delve too deeply into the psychosexual fundaments of your relationship. Rather, concentrate on your mate's career and business life; here's where you can give him or her the push that is needed. Be tough while at the same time you boost their confidence. Sexually and affectionally, you should be consistent in your attentions. A splurge-and-stint approach will bewilder your Cancer lover, closing that protective shell even tighter. Be totally open with your Cancer mate, for she or he will thrive on understanding and comforting you.

ARIES—LEO

A strong bond exists between you two. Once you have survived the wars waged by your egos, it will be hard to pry you apart emotionally. You are both idealistic, emotional creatures governed by the power of creation and the love of life. Love is your great source of energy, and you cannot be without it. When you are together and in love, your capacity to love each other (as well as yourselves) is limitless. Self-involved and demanding, you can have raging battles yet somehow remain loyal through it all. You can be adventurous and passionate, and can make a glamorous couple.

Ambitious and dynamic, you are both imbued with the fighting spirit and a joy of living that makes whatever you do radiant with the strength of your combined spirit. Whatever you dedicate yourselves to as a team will doubtless be a success, provided selfishness and ego don't expand faster than your mutual understanding. Leo may play the baby for a long, long time, but Aries will still be in love—tantrums, flirtations, and bossiness notwithstanding. Leo is grateful for that strong Aries influence, which can help make dreams come true, and can take new chances in life.

Hints for Your Leo Mate

Accent your alliance with all the loving gestures that make the proud Lion feel secure and wanted. Affectionately tease him or her; make a friendly fuss, not a bossy one, if you Aries want to keep your Leo mate happy. Never chastise Leo in a way that hurts the pride. A lot of backpatting will substitute for frank appraisals of what you feel is not being handled appropriately. You must respect Leo's need to keep a relatively private ego; unlike you, your Leo lover is not talkative or prone to use words to control a situation. Chances are Leo will welcome your passions as much as he or she expresses their own, so you do not have to repress your emotional nature. Nevertheless Leo expects you to be the idea person you are, and the route to compatibility is through the heart to the head. Stress the individuality of your lives with each other, for each of you is a leader. If you must divert Leo's demands upon you, talk about your needs and problems; nothing flatters your mate more than being asked to mother you.

ARIES—VIRGO

You two have very different perspectives, approaches, and philosophies. Yet you are probably curious about each other, feeling distant but still attracted in some strange way. It could be years before you ever really get to know each other, for you both require separateness to develop your individual beings. Neither of you is interested in relating constantly or revealing too much about yourselves, although you will often remain faithful in a personal relationship. But to make this work you both need to exert some sustained efforts at adjustment.

You will sometimes be the cause of separation and strife, since the assertion of independence is fundamental to your Aries personality. When your Virgo is hurt, you will see a retreat into coldness. That detached unreachability will frustrate and challenge you. Once inflamed, you can chase, court, win over. And the cycle begins again.

Virgo's shy approach is seductive, but Victorian attitudes can be a drag indeed. Your verve as an Aries is your inspiration, but impetuosity and aggressiveness repel a quiet Virgo nature. Success in this relationship depends upon the right blend of action and propriety. If you start out with mutual respect and trust, you will be giving yourselves the best insurance. Earthy practicality, discipline, and diligence can join with the daring zest of taking a chance on life and being successful.

Hints for Your Virgo Mate

Respect and interest will win the heart of your basically aloof Virgo mate. Be dutiful in small ways. Be grand in large ways. Conduct yourself with more aplomb than flamboyance, dressing for the occasion and affecting a casual demeanor, thereby pleasing your impeccable partner; let Virgo be the intense one. Introduce variety into your relationship by exciting plans for travel, work and community projects, education that can be shared. Skillfully guide your Virgo mate to assume and execute responsibilities. Sympathize with his or her problems. Listen patiently to the complaints and the analysis, agree with the value judgments, then gently nudge her or him back to whatever task seemed so onerous to begin with. When your Virgo partner criticizes you, accept it as constructive analysis. Do something tangible—don't just bolt. A small gesture proves its point but doesn't compromise your vision. Don't take your Virgo mate for granted; be attentive, but not sticky or silly.

ARIES—LIBRA

You have both been under heavy stress ever since the last decade. Unexpected reversals, changes, and removals have characterized your lives, and partnerships have taken unusual turns. It's a question of independence, really, and reflects basic questions about human commitments, the ability to form lasting unions, and the desire to cooperate with each other. Role playing in the sexual and emotional sides of the relationship has probably occurred.

Active or passive, aggressive or shy, independent or dependent, you have both learned how to cope with disruption, separation, and strange reversals. You now know how important it is to have a separate life in order to avoid exhausting the resources of the relationship. Each of you is still seeking to find your true self—who you are, defined by you, on your own terms. If you wrap yourself up totally in your partner, and plan all your life around one person, you may resent it and lose your self-esteem and confidence. Yet to destroy a good relationship can take away one of your major joys in living. Aim to blend self-fulfillment with the capacity to cooperate. Independence, equality, and awareness must characterize a long period of change and growth.

Hints for Your Libra Mate

You may sometimes be at a loss to understand your Libra mate, who revels in the moody and fluid side of their planetary ruler, Venus. Although words and talk are a large part of your sharing and good feeling, the actions that follow mutual disclosures seem to be incongruous, often contradictory. At such times, repress your need to confront, challenge, force change. Your Libra mate flees from conflict; the merest suggestion of a flawed performance pressures Libra to run. Go with your mate's moods, though never losing sight of your real goals. In the context of enlightened conversation, you can air all passions and grievances. As long as Libra feels the goal is mutual, your mate will work toward it. Be protective yet decisive; your Libra partner wants to participate in decision making, but may not be able to make quick and independent decisions, as you can. Parties and people are important to your Libra lover; generously supply both in your lives together. Allowing your Libra mate to take the lead in fashioning the social atmosphere will always earn you points and commitment.

ARIES—SCORPIO

This is an exciting (and dangerous) combination. You'll make Scorpio work for it, and your Scorpio will excite you deep down at the most primitive levels of your being. Instead of turning your energies against each other and developing a diabolical and constantly escalating war, try to work toward mutual inspiration on sexual, emotional, and creative levels.

You share the primary instincts for being: survival, life, death. When it comes to ambition, energy, and stamina, together you are unbeatable. You are both stubborn and strong-willed. You have conflicting views of openness and secrecy, freedom and control, but when you cooperate and don't get in each other's way, it's a dynamic combination.

You can be a couple of magicians, mystic sorcerers with a love for the mysterious. Together, your power of leadership, creativity, renewal, and regeneration can build a whole new world. Your collisions are explosive and exciting. The product of those eruptions could be enough light and energy to launch a thousand ships. At best, you are a deep and lasting alliance, resilient, indestructible, and powerful.

Hints for Your Scorpio Mate

You two Mars creatures certainly can give each other a run for the money. Both of you need to dominate, but your Scorpio's need is deep and abiding. Thwarted, it can turn to resentment or a malevolent form of retaliation. Fortunately you can give up the driver's seat and restrain your independent streak often enough to mollify your Scorpio lover. Play down your own flippancy, but don't let Scorpio's sarcasm rile you into attack. Harmless flirting or showing too much interest in other people will arouse wild jealousy. You must be a totally committed lover. And don't use words as a substitute for that strong, silent sexuality Scorpio wants to elicit from you. If you hope to preserve the relationship as well as your independent strengths, set up separate but equal domains. The best strategy when Scorpio retreats into that moody secretiveness is calm acceptance. Verbal confrontations or forcing your mate into action only engender strife. Setting a pace for relaxation and introspection will work wonders. Without being childish, allow your Scorpio mate to be protective of you.

ARIES—SAGITTARIUS

This is a strong love match. Sagittarius loves that Aries spirit, and you can light each other's fires with your passion for living life to the fullest. You can lift each other's hearts with a buoyancy and thrust that other less fiery types of people will envy and admire. You may have a time living with each other, since you can share a restlessness, blind idealism, or vain self-involvement that will irk each of you about your partner before long. You reflect each other's egotism royally.

Either one of you could fly off on a thousand tangents, never meeting, never really completing your connection. You could be terrible influences on each other, stimulating a lawlessness or thoughtlessness that can lead nowhere. Without practical discipline and methods your plans—in fact, your whole relationship—could never get off the drawing board.

You both share a fundamental joy, a love for adventure, and a hankering after new experiences. Your positive approach to life gives a healthy, lusty swing to everything you do, and together you are full of momentum, resilience, and energy. You are both freedom lovers and can raise each other to great heights of learning and travel and wisdom. Your turn Sagittarius on physically and as a creative inspired personality, blending energy and enthusiasm in the relationship.

Hints for Your Sagittarius Mate

Remember how exciting, spontaneous, and adventurous your courtship was? Keep up that happy acceptance of your Sagittarius mate and there never will be cause for your partnership to suffer. Don't try to pin your mate down to executing all the ideas she or he has shared with you. Great idealists, nevertheless your Sagittarius partner experiences some discomfort actually getting things done. Now you can't be too bossy in this regard, but you can be a controlling force without making Sagittarius feel their freedom is lost. Although your mate will pioneer ideas with you, you must be the one to initiate the action. You must also lay a gentle restraining hand on your mate, who can be even more reckless than you. Sagittarius loves arguments, so open a variety of topics to fire your mate's heart and mind. Share your partner's love of sports and the outdoors, a robust life of recreation and activity. You may wind up being more the homemaker and money manager than your mate, who will love you eternally for assuming these responsibilities.

ARIES—CAPRICORN

With your creativity, zest, and superconfidence and Capricorn's patience, method, and determination, your union has all the basics for success. You have the driving force and Capricorn has the way with people. Together you can accomplish the impossible. Of course, you will think it takes too long, and Capricorn will think it's a little harebrained or crazy, but when you put your heads together to confer or conspire, the result is the successful execution of any Herculean task.

Tension will be great in such a relationship, since the fire of your Aries spirit must submit to the cool, practical approach of Capricorn stability. Capricorn's need for control will be upset by your stubborn independence and refusal to knuckle under to facts. Without understanding and a mutual desire for growth, your relationship could come to a frustrating stalemate, a deadlock that even time cannot solve.

Despite the professional battles and crisis situations of the past few years, you can weather the storms for the purpose of sharing your goals. You both need sustenance and security. Any burdens or responsibilities that circumstances impose on your lives can help you grow closer and more determined to make the relationship succeed through loving each other.

Hints for Your Capricorn Mate

You, the Ram, and your Capricorn mate, the Goat, have a lot in common, so when you want to please him or her, do it the way you would please yourself. It's most important to support your mate's career and life goals; the ambitions of a Capricorn loom mightily. At the same time, show your partner how responsible you are to your own work and outside interests. In fact, let her or him in on your goals as well as your friendship circle. Your Capricorn mate will love you for the opportunity to give sound advice. As long as you are an admiring lover and a stable homemaker, your irascible moods won't bother your Capricorn partner. Of course, you cannot go dashing around starting things but not following through. And don't be sloppy or insensitive; your mate abhors anything in bad taste. Sometimes you will have to push the Goat into action, to overcome your lover's shyness and fear of failure. Be bold and daring, and your Capricorn mate will have found the perfect partner.

ARIES—AQUARIUS

You may meet out of nowhere and strike up a full-blown friendship. You may develop a long-lasting spiritual relationship of support and mutual understanding, making valuable contributions to each other's lives. A successful partnership for you two might seem strange to the people around you, for it will probably be a volatile blend of independence and bohemianism. If you try to make your life simple, and free it from traditional jealousies and cloying attachments, you can make the relationship work. You need innovation, change, and excitement in your union. The element of surprise will keep fanning the flame of this zany match.

When the newness wears off, you could fall out of each other's lives as fast as you fell in. When jealousy and possessiveness replace spontaneity and respect for each other's way, sudden flare-ups and explosive confrontations can threaten your peace and even do irreparable damage to a growing and fruitful friendship. Involvements are getting more powerful now. New emotional and sexual scenes may be tipping the scales. Experimentalism and self-will can bring separations to this relationship—or they can bring greater growth through meeting an explosive and exciting time.

Hints for Your Aquarius Mate

Freedom and friendship are keys for a successful partnership. You can be as free as you like as long as you do not curtail the activities or censor the thoughts of your Aquarius mate. Even if you have passed the courtship stage, the emphasis should still be on the experimental and the radical. Don't stampede your lover's affections. A challenge to Aquarius unpredictability will make them even more moody and perverse than is the rule. And don't put stock in convention or routine; allow your Aquarius to be late, to miss appointments, to change plans. You can do this, too, and the more surprises you deliver to your Aquarius lover, the more loved you will be. Your recklessness with ideas and projects—not money—will appeal to your partner. Don't demand too much passion in your sexual relationship. The real delving in this partnership is in and of the mind. So focus your insight and vision on your Aquarius mate's intellectual capacities; stir her or him to express thoughts, feelings, and hopes.

ARIES—PISCES

This is a strange and mysterious combination. Yours is a fascinating challenge, since neither of you is terribly realistic and both of you have to learn about life through experience—often the hard way. Together you can know the meaning of a love that you may have thought impossible to achieve on Earth. You may be disillusioned and disappointed, having to start over again and again, forgiving and escaping, and forgiving again. You could find yourselves in a horribly perplexing situation. Together, you blend verve, enthusiasm, and sensitivity with guilty uncertainty. You can play on each other's guilt and sense of responsibility and can founder in deception and worry.

But your lives can be illuminated by gentle, devotional love, enhanced by poetry, music, and a spiritual understanding that can raise your mutual spirits out of the ordinary problems of personal relationships. Your passions are deep. Your desires for pleasure may excite the wildest parts of your lives together or can send you both fleeing in opposite directions. Being resilient takes you out of worry and confusion. Compassion and forgiveness awaken your sense of the other's needs and deepen the relationship between you.

Hints for Your Pisces Mate

You are almost complete opposites, but Pisces, the sign of the Fishes, has a double personality, so your relating to each other is even more complicated. Never be bewildered by your Pisces mate's emotional displays. Appreciate that need for drama, and be up to playing the antagonist in her or his movie. You can even play the villain—as long as you react! In real life matters, the situation is different, and you can be entirely yourself, doing what you do best: decide, direct, and drive, even if it feels like dragging your dreamy lover along. Don't criticize Pisces for inconsistency or laziness. Rather get him or her on a path and out of yours. Sometimes you should be more accepting of the dreamer that your Pisces partner is; tune in to the intuitive vibes, experience the melancholy and rapture for yourself. Encourage your lover's interest in the arts. Grace the relationship with Pisces by such thoughtful gestures as flowers, notes, surprise gifts.

ARIES:
YOUR PROGRESSED SUN

WHAT IS YOUR NEW SIGN?

Your birth sign, or Sun sign, is the central core of your whole personality. It symbolizes everything you try to do and be. It is your main streak, your major source of power, vitality, and life. But as you live you learn, and as you learn you progress. The element in your horoscope that measures your progress is called the Progressed Sun. It is the symbol of your growth on Earth, and represents new threads that run through your life. The Progressed Sun measures big changes, turning points, and major decisions. It will often describe the path you are making toward the development of your personality and the fulfillment of your desires.

Below you will find brief descriptions of the Progressed Sun in three signs. According to the table on page 43, find out about your Progressed Sun and see how and where you fit into the cosmic scheme. Each period lasts about 30 years, so watch and see how dramatic these changes turn out to be.

If Your Sun Is Progressing Into—

TAURUS, you begin to acquire possessions and wake up to your earthly needs. Money enters your life in a significant way. Though your fantasies grow richer, you need to develop your earthy sense of values. You want to earn your own way and be paid for your efforts.

GEMINI, you begin to move out, get around, and start contacting the people around you. You enter into a period of communication with everyone around you. Involvements with relatives and neighbors will occupy much of your time. Your curiosity will be ever whetted.

CANCER, you will now begin to feel a need to put down roots and seek the peace of your own private haven. You will tend to be a little withdrawn during this period of your life. Connections with the family will play a major role in all your activities, for good or ill, and you will find yourself more ready to accept attachments and dependencies than ever before.

HOW TO USE THE TABLE

Look for your birthday in the table on the facing page; then under the appropriate column, find out approximately when your Progressed Sun will lead you to a new sign. From that point on, for 30 years, the thread of your life will run through that sign. Read the definitions on the preceding pages and see exactly how that life thread will develop.

For example, if your birthday is March 24, your Progressed Sun will enter Taurus around your 27th birthday and will travel through Taurus until you are 57 years old. Your Progressed Sun will then move into Gemini. Reading the definitions of Taurus and Gemini will tell you much about your major involvements and interests during those years.

YOUR PROGRESSED SUN

If your birthday falls on	start looking at TAURUS at age	start looking at GEMINI at age	start looking at CANCER at age
March 20–21	30	60	90
22	29	59	89
23	28	58	88
24	27	57	87
25	26	56	86
26	25	55	85
27	24	54	84
28	23	53	83
29	22	52	82
30	21	51	81
31	20	50	80
April 1	19	49	79
2	18	48	78
3	17	47	77
4	16	46	76
5	15	45	75
6	14	44	74
7	13	43	73
8	12	42	72
9	11	41	71
10	10	40	70
11	9	39	69
12	8	38	68
13	7	37	67
14	6	36	66
15	5	35	65
16	4	34	64
17	3	33	63
18	2	32	62
19	1	31	61

ARIES BIRTHDAYS

March 21	Otis Spann, Phyllis McGinley
March 22	Rosa Bonheur, Marcel Marceau
March 23	Dane Rudhyar, Joan Crawford
March 24	Wilhelm Reich, Clyde Barrow
March 25	Aretha Franklin, Gloria Steinem
March 26	Tennessee Williams, Diana Ross
March 27	Sarah Vaughan
March 28	Edmund Muskie
March 29	Pearl Bailey
March 30	Van Gogh, Warren Beatty
March 31	Descartes, Richard Chamberlain
April 1	Bach, Lon Chaney, Debbie Reynolds
April 2	Hans Christian Andersen, Casanova
April 3	Marlon Brando, Doris Day
April 4	Arthur Murray, Maya Angelou
April 5	Spencer Tracy, Bette Davis
April 6	Lowell Thomas, Baba Ram Dass
April 7	Walter Winchell
April 8	Billie Holiday
April 9	W.C. Fields, Paul Robeson
April 10	Omar Sharif, Clare Booth Luce
April 11	Charles Evans Hughes
April 12	David Cassidy, Ann Miller
April 13	Thomas Jefferson, Eudora Welty
April 14	Julie Christie
April 15	Leonardo Da Vinci, Bessie Smith
April 16	Wilbur Wright, Polly Adler
April 17	William Holden, J. P. Morgan
April 18	Leopold Stokowski, Hayley Mills
April 19	Hugh O'Brien, Jayne Mansfield
April 20	Miró, Nina Foch

CAN ASTROLOGY PREDICT THE FUTURE?

Can astrology really peer into the future? By studying the planets and the stars is it possible to look years ahead and make predictions for our lives? How can we draw the line between ignorant superstition and cosmic mystery? We live in a very civilized world, to be sure. We consider ourselves modern, enlightened individuals. Yet few of us can resist the temptation to take a peek at the future when we think it's possible. Why? What is the basis of such universal curiosity?

The answer is simple. Astrology works, and you don't have to be a magician to find that out. We certainly can't prove astrology simply by taking a look at the astonishing number of people who believe in it, but such figures do make us wonder what lies behind such widespread popularity. Everywhere in the world hundreds of thousands of serious, intelligent people are charting, studying, and interpreting the positions of the planets and stars every day. Every facet of the media dispenses daily astrological bulletins to millions of curious seekers. In Eastern countries, the source of many wisdoms handed down to us from antiquity, astrology still has a vital place. Why? Surrounded as we are by sophisticated scientific method, how does astrology, with all its bizarre symbolism and mysterious meaning, survive so magnificently? The answer remains the same. It works.

Nobody knows exactly where astrological knowledge came from. We have references to it dating back to the dawn of human history. Wherever there was a stirring of human consciousness, people began to observe the natural cycles and rhythms that sustained their life. The diversity of human behavior must have been evident even to the first students of consciousness. Yet the basic similarity between members of the human family must have led to the search for some common source, some greater point of origin somehow linked to the heavenly bodies ruling our sense of life and time. The ancient world of Mesopotamia, Chaldea, and Egypt was a highly developed center of astronomical observation and astrological interpretation of heavenly phenomena and their resultant effects on human life.

Amid the seeming chaos of a mysterious unknown universe, people from earliest times sought to classify, define, and organize the world around them. Order: that's what the human mind has always striven to maintain in an unceasing battle with its natural counterpart, chaos, or entropy. We build cities, countries, and empires, subjugating nature to a point of near defeat, and then . . . civilization collapses, empires fall, and cities crumble. Nature reclaims the wilderness. Shelly's poem *Ozymandias* is a hymn to the battle between order and chaos. The narrator tells us about a statue, broken, shattered, and half-sunk somewhere in the middle of a distant desert. The inscription reads: "Look on my works, ye mighty, and despair." And then we are told: "Nothing beside remains. Round the decay of that colossal wreck, boundless and bare, the lone and level sands stretch far away."

People always feared the entropy that seemed to lurk in nature. So we found permanence and constancy in the regular movements of the Sun, Moon, and planets and in the positions of the stars. Traditions sprang up from observations of the seasons and crops. Relationships were noted between phenomena in nature and the configurations of the heavenly bodies. This "synchronicity," as it was later called by Carl Jung, extended to thought, mood, and behavior, and as such developed the astrological archetypes handed down to us today.

Astrology, a regal science of the stars in the old days, was made available to the king, who was informed of impending events in the heavens, translated of course to their earthly meanings by trusted astrologers. True, astrological knowledge in its infant stages was rudimentary and beset with many superstitions and false premises. But those same dangers exist today in any investigation of occult or mystical subjects. In the East, reverence for astrology is part of religion. Astrologer-astronomers have held respected positions in government and have taken part in advisory councils on many momentous issues. The duties of the court astrologer, whose office was one of the most important in the land, were clearly defined, as early records show.

Here in our sleek Western world, astrology glimmers on, perhaps more brilliantly than ever. With all of our technological wonders and complex urbanized environments, we look to astrology even now to cut through artificiality, dehumanization, and all the materialism of contemporary life, while we gather precious information that helps us live in that material world. Astrology helps us restore balance and get in step with our own rhythms and the rhythms of nature.

Intelligent investigation of astrology (or the practical application of it) need not mean blind acceptance. We only need to see it working, see our own lives confirming its principles every day, in order to accept and understand it more. To understand ourselves is to know ourselves and to know all. This book can help you to do that—to understand yourself and through understanding develop your own resources and potentials as a rich human being.

YOUR PLACE AMONG THE STARS

Humanity finds itself at the center of a vast personal universe that extends infinitely outward in all directions. In that sense each is a kind of star radiating, as our Sun does, to all bodies everywhere. These vibrations, whether loving, helpful, or destructive, extend outward and generate a kind of "atmosphere" in which woman and man move. The way we relate to everything around us—our joy or our sorrow—becomes a living part of us. Our loved ones and our enemies become the objects of our projected radiations, for better or worse. Our bodies and faces reflect thoughts and emotions much the way light from the Sun reflects the massive reactions occurring deep within its interior. This energy and light reach all who enter its sphere of influence.

Our own personal radiations are just as potent in their own way, really. The reactions that go on deep within us profoundly affect our way of thinking and acting. Our feelings of joy or satisfaction, frustration or anger, must eventually find an outlet. Otherwise we experience the psychological or physiological repercussions of repression. If we can't have a good cry, tell someone our troubles, or express love, we soon feel very bad indeed.

As far as our physical selves are concerned, there is a direct relationship between our outer lives, inner reactions and actions, and the effects on our physical body. We all know the feeling of being startled by the sudden ring of a telephone, or the simple frustration of missing a bus. In fact, our minds and bodies are constantly reacting to outside forces. At the same time we, too, are generating actions that will cause a reaction in someone else. You may suddenly decide to phone a friend. If you are a bus driver you might speed along on your way and leave behind an angry would-be passenger. Whatever the case, mind and body are in close communication and they both reflect each other's condition. Next time you're really angry take a good long look in the mirror!

In terms of human evolution, our ability to understand, control, and ultimately change ourselves will naturally affect all of our outside relationships. Astrology is invaluable to helping us comprehend our inner selves. It is a useful tool in helping us retain our integrity, while cooperating with and living in a world full of other human beings.

Let's go back to our original question: Can astrology predict the future? To know that, we must come to an understanding of what the future is.

In simplest terms the future is the natural next step to the present, just as the present is a natural progression from the past. Although our minds can move from one to the other, there is a thread of continuity between past, present, and future that joins them together in a coherent sequence. If you are reading this book at this moment, it is the result of a real conscious choice you made in the recent past. That is, you chose to find out what was on these pages, picked up the book, and opened it. Because of this choice you may know yourself better in the future. It's as simple as that.

Knowing ourselves is the key to being able to predict and understand our own future. To learn from past experiences, choices, and actions is to fully grasp the present. Coming to grips with the present is to be master of the future.

"Know thyself" is a motto that takes us back to the philosophers of ancient Greece. Mystery religions and cults of initiation throughout the ancient world, schools of mystical discipline, yoga and mental expansion have always been guardians of this one sacred phrase. Know thyself. Of course, that's easy to say. But how do you go about it when there are so many conflicts in our lives and different parts of our personalities? How do we know when we are really "being ourselves" and not merely being influenced by the things we read or see on television, or by the people around us? How can we differentiate the various parts of our character and still remain whole?

There are many methods of classifying human beings into types. Body shapes, muscular types, blood types, and genetic types are only a few. Psychology has its own ways of classifying human beings according to their behavior. Anthropology studies human evolution as the body-mind response to environment. Biology watches physical development and adaptations in body structure. These fields provide valuable information about human beings and the ways they survive, grow, and change in their search for their place in eternity. Yet these branches of science have been separate and fragmented. Their contribution has been to provide theories and data, yes, but no lasting solutions to the human problems that have existed since the first two creatures realized they had two separate identities.

It's often difficult to classify yourself according to these different schemes. It's not easy to be objective about yourself. Some things are hard to face; others are hard to see. The different perspectives afforded to us by studying the human organism from all these different disciplines may seem contradictory when they are all really trying to integrate humankind into the whole of the cosmic scheme.

Astrology can help these disciplines unite to seek a broader and deeper approach to universal human issues. Astrology's point of view is vast. It transcends racial, ethnic, genetic, environmental, and even historical criteria, yet somehow includes them all. Astrology embraces the totality of human experience, then sets about to examine the relationships that are created within that experience.

We don't simply say, "The planets cause this or that." Rather than merely isolating cause or effect, astrology has unified the ideas of cause and effect. Concepts of past, present, and future merge and become, as we shall see a little later on, like stepping-stones across the great stream of mind. Observations of people and the environment have developed the astrological principles of planetary "influence," but it must be remembered that if there is actual influence, it is mutual. As the planets influence us, so we influence them, for we are forever joined to all past and future motion of the heavenly bodies. This is the foundation of astrology as it has been built up over the centuries.

ORDER VS. CHAOS

But is it all written in the stars? Is it destined that empires should thrive and flourish, kings reign, lovers love, and then . . . decay, ruin, and natural disintegration hold sway? Have we anything to do with determining the cycles of order and chaos? The art of the true astrologer depends on his ability to uncover new information, place it upon the grid of data already collected, and then interpret what he sees as accurate probability in human existence. There may be a paradox here. If we can predict that birds will fly south, could we not, with enough time and samples for observation, determine their ultimate fate when they arrive in the south?

The paradox is that there is no paradox at all. Order and chaos exist together simultaneously in one observable universe. At some remote point in time and space the Earth was formed, and for one reason or another, life appeared here. Whether the appearance of life on planets is a usual phenomenon or an unrepeated accident we can only speculate at this moment. But our

Earth and all living things upon its surface conform to certain laws of physical materiality that our observations have led us to write down and contemplate. All creatures, from the one-celled ameba to a man hurrying home at rush hour, have some basic traits in common. Life in its organization goes from the simple to the complex with a perfection and order that is both awesome and inspiring. If there were no order to our physical world, an apple could turn into a worm and cows could be butterflies.

But the world is an integrated whole, unified with every other part of creation. When nature does take an unexpected turn, we call that a mutation. This is the exciting card in the program of living experience that tells us not everything is written at all. Spontaneity is real. Change is real. Freedom from the expected norm is real. We have seen in nature that only those mutations that can adapt to changes in their environment and continue reproducing themselves will survive. But possibilities are open for sudden transformation, and that keeps the whole world growing.

FREE CHOICE AND
THE VALUE OF PREDICTIONS

Now it's time to turn our attention to the matter of predictions. That was our original question after all: Can astrology peer into the future? Well, astrological prognostication is an awe-inspiring art and requires deep philosophical consideration before it is to be undertaken. Not only are there many grids that must be laid one upon the other before such predictions can be made, but there are ethical issues that plague every student of the stars. How much can you really see? How much should you tell? What is the difference between revealing valuable data and disclosing negative or harmful programing?

If an astrologer tells you only the good things, you'll have little confidence in the analysis when you are passing through crisis. On the other hand, if the astrologer is a prophet of doom who can see nothing but the dark clouds on the horizon, you will eventually have to reject astrology because you will come to associate it with the bad luck in your life.

Astrology itself is beyond any practitioner's capacity to grasp it all. Unrealistic utopianism or gloomy determinism reflect not the truth of astrology but the truth of the astrologer interpreting what he sees. In order to solve problems and make accurate predictions, you have to be *able* to look on the dark side of things without dwelling there. You have to be able to take a look at all the possibilities, all the possible meanings of a certain planetary influence without jumping to premature conclusions. Objective scanning and assessment take much practice and great skill.

No matter how skilled the astrologer is, he cannot assume the responsibility for your life. Only you can take that responsibility as your life unfolds. In a way, the predictions of this book are glancing ahead up the road, much the way a road map can indicate turns up ahead this way or that. You, however, are still driving the car.

What, then, is a horoscope? If it is a picture of you at your moment of birth, are you then frozen forever in time and space, unable to budge or deviate from the harsh, unyielding declarations of the stars? Not at all.

The universe is always in motion. Each moment follows the moment before it. As the present is the result of all past choices and action, so the future is the result of today's choices. But if we can go to a planetary calendar and see where planets will be located two years from now, then how can individual free choice exist? This is a question that has haunted authors and philosophers since the first thinkers recorded their thoughts. In the end, of course, we must all reason things out for ourselves and come to our own conclusions. It is easy to be impressed or influenced by people who seem to know a lot more than we do, but in reality we must all find codes of beliefs with which we are the most comfortable.

But if we can stretch our imaginations up, up above the line of time as it exists from one point to another, we can almost see past, present, and future, all together. We can almost feel this vibrant thread of creative free choice that pushes forward at every moment, actually causing the future to happen! Free will, that force that changes the entire course of a stream, exists within the stream of mind itself—the collective mind, or intelligence, of humanity. Past, present, and future are mere stepping-stones across that great current.

Our lives continue a thread of an intelligent mind that existed before we were born and will exist after we die. It is like an endless relay race. At birth we pick up a torch and carry it, lighting the way with that miraculous light of consciousness of immortality. Then we pass it on to others when we die. What we call the *unconscious* may be part of this great stream of mind, which learns and shares experiences with everything that has ever lived or will ever live on this world or any other.

Yet we all come to Earth with different family circumstances, backgrounds, and characteristics. We all come to life with different planetary configurations. Indeed each person *is* different, yet we are all the same. We have different tasks or responsibilities or lifestyles, but underneath we share a common current—the powerful stream of human intelligence. Each of us has different sets of circumstances to deal with because of the choices he or she has made in the past. We all possess different assets and have different resources to fall back on, weaknesses to strengthen, and sides of our nature to transform. We are all what we are now because of what we were before. The present is the sum of the past. And we will be what we will be in the future because of what we are now.

It is foolish to pretend that there are no specific boundaries or limitations to any of our particular lives. Family background, racial, cultural, or religious indoctrinations, physical characteristics, these are all inescapable facts of our being that must be incorporated and accepted into our maturing mind. But each person possesses the capacity for breakthrough, forgiveness, and total transformation. It has taken millions of years since people first began to walk upright. We cannot expect an overnight evolution to take place. There are many things about our personalities that are very much like our parents. Sometimes that thought makes us uncomfortable, but it's true.

It's also true that we are not our parents. You are *you*, just you, and nobody else but you. That's one of the wondrous aspects of astrology. The levels on which each planetary configuration works out will vary from individual to individual. Often an aspect of selfishness will be manifested in one person, yet in another it may appear as sacrifice and kindness.

Development is inevitable in human consciousness. But the direction of that development is not. As plants will bend toward the light as they grow, so there is the possibility for the human mind to grow toward the light of integrity and truth. The Age of Aquarius that everyone is talking about must first take place within each human's mind and heart. An era of peace, freedom, and community cannot be legislated by any government, no matter how liberal. It has to be a spontaneous flow of human spirit and fellowship. It will be a magnificent dawning on the globe of consciousness that reflects the joy of the human heart to be part of the great stream of intelligence and love. It must be generated by an enlightened, realistic humanity. There's no law that can put it into effect, no magic potion to drink that will make it all come true. It will be the result of all people's efforts to assume their personal and social responsibilities and to carve out a new destiny for humankind.

As you read the predictions in this book, bear in mind that they have been calculated by means of planetary positions for whole groups of people. Thus their value lies in your ability to coordinate what you read with the nature of your life's circumstances at the present time. You have seen how many complex relationships must be analyzed in individual horoscopes before sensible accurate conclusions can be drawn. No matter what the indications, a person has his or her own life, own intelligence, basic native strength that must ultimately be the source of action and purpose. When you are living truthfully and in harmony with what you know is right, there are no forces, threats, or obstacles that can defeat you.

With these predictions, read the overall pattern and see how rhythms begin to emerge. They are not caused by remote alien forces, millions of miles out in space.

You and the planets are one. What you do, they do. What they do, you do. But can you change their course? No, but you cannot change many of your basic characteristics either. Still, within that already existing framework, you are the master. You can still differentiate between what is right for you and what is not. You can seize opportunities and act on them, you can create beauty and seek love.

The purpose of looking ahead is not to scare yourself. Look ahead to enlarge your perspective, enhance your overall view of the life *you* are developing. Difficult periods cause stress certainly, but at the same time they give you the chance to reassess your condition, restate and redefine exactly what is important to you, so you can cherish your life more. Joyous periods should be lived to the fullest with the happiness and exuberance that each person richly deserves.

YOUR HOROSCOPE AND THE ZODIAC

It's possible that in your own body, as you read this passage, there exist atoms as old as time itself. You could well be the proud possessor of some carbon and hydrogen (two necessary elements in the development of life) that came into being in the heart of a star billions and billions of years ago. That star could have exploded and cast its matter far into space. This matter could have formed another star, and then another, until finally our Sun was born. From the Sun's nuclear reactions came the material that later formed the planets—and maybe some of that primeval carbon or hydrogen. That material could have become part of the Earth, part of an early ocean, even early life. These same atoms could well have been carried down to the present day, to this very moment as you read this book. It's really quite possible. You can see how everything is linked to everything else. Our Earth now exists in a gigantic universe that showers it constantly with rays and invisible particles. You are the point into which all these energies and influences have been focused. You are the prism through which all the light of outer space is being refracted. You are literally a reflection of all the planets and stars.

Your horoscope is a picture of the sky at the moment of your birth. It's like a gigantic snapshot of the positions of the planets and stars, taken from Earth. Of course, the planets never stop moving around the Sun even for the briefest moment, and you represent that motion as it was occurring at the exact hour of your birth at the precise location on the Earth where you were born.

When an astrologer is going to read your chart, he or she asks you for the month, day, and year of your birth. She also needs the exact time and place. With this information he sets about consulting various charts and tables in his calculation of the specific positions of the Sun, Moon, and stars, relative to your birthplace when you came to Earth. Then he or she locates them by means of the *Zodiac*.

The Zodiac is a group of stars, centered against the Sun's apparent path around the Earth, and these star groups are divided into twelve equal segments, or *signs*. What we are actually dividing up is the Earth's path around the Sun. But from our point of view here on Earth, it seems as if the Sun is making a great circle around our planet in the sky, so we say it's the Sun's apparent path. This twelvefold division, the Zodiac, is like a mammoth address system for any body in the sky. At any given moment, the planets can all be located at a specific point along this path.

Now where are you in this system? First you look to your *Sun sign*—the section of the Zodiac that the Sun occupied when you were born. A great part of your character, in fact the central thread of your whole being, is described by your Sun sign. Each sign of the Zodiac has certain basic traits associated with it. Since the Sun remains in each sign for about thirty days, that divides the population into twelve major character types. Of course, not everybody born the same month will have the same character, but you'll be amazed at how many fundamental traits you share with your astrological cousins of the same birth sign, no matter how many environmental differences you boast.

The dates on which the Sun sign changes will vary from year to year. That is why some people born near the *cusp*, or edge, of a sign have difficulty determining their true birth sign without the aid of an astrologer who can plot precisely the Sun's apparent motion (the Earth's motion) for any given year. But to help you find your true Sun sign, a Table of Cusp Dates for the years 1900 to 2010 is provided for you on page 17.

Here are the twelve signs of the Zodiac as western astrology has recorded them. Listed also are the symbols associated with them and the *approximate* dates when the Sun enters and exits each sign for the year 2007.

Aries	Ram	March 20–April 20
Taurus	Bull	April 20–May 21
Gemini	Twins	May 21–June 21
Cancer	Crab	June 21–July 23
Leo	Lion	July 23–August 23
Virgo	Virgin	August 23–September 23
Libra	Scales	September 23–October 23
Scorpio	Scorpion	October 23–November 22
Sagittarius	Archer	November 22–December 22
Capricorn	Sea Goat	December 22–January 20
Aquarius	Water Bearer	January 20–February 18
Pisces	Fish	February 18–March 20

In a horoscope the *Rising sign*, or Ascendant, is often considered to be as important as the Sun sign. In a later chapter (see pages 82–84) the Rising sign is discussed in detail. But to help you determine your own Rising sign, a Table of Rising Signs is provided for you on pages 20–21.

THE SIGNS OF THE ZODIAC

The signs of the Zodiac are an ingenious and complex summary of human behavioral and physical types, handed down from generation to generation through the bodies of all people in their hereditary material and through their minds. On the following pages you will find brief descriptions of all twelve signs in their highest and most ideal expression.

ARIES
The Sign of the Ram

Aries is the first sign of the Zodiac, and marks the beginning of springtime and the birth of the year. In spring the Earth begins its ascent upward and tips its North Pole toward the Sun. During this time the life-giving force of the Sun streams toward Earth, bathing our planet with the kiss of warmth and life. Plants start growing. Life wakes up. No more waiting. No more patience. The message has come from the Sun: Time to live!

Aries is the sign of the Self and is the crusade for the right of an individual to live in unimpeachable freedom. It represents the supremacy of the human will over all obstacles, limitations, and threats. In Aries there is unlimited energy, optimism, and daring, for it is the pioneer in search of a new world. It is the story of success and renewal, championship, and victory. It is the living spirit of resilience and the power to be yourself, free from all restrictions and conditioning. There is no pattern you *have* to repeat, nobody's rule you *have* to follow.

Confidence and positive action are born in Aries, with little thought or fear of the past. Life is as magic as sunrise, with all the creative potential ahead of you for a new day. Activity, energy, and adventure characterize this sign. In this sector of the Zodiac there is amazing strength, forthrightness, honesty, and a stubborn refusal to accept defeat. The Aries nature is forgiving, persuasive, masterful, and decisive.

In short, Aries is the magic spark of life and being, the source of all initiative, courage, independence, and self-esteem.

TAURUS
The Sign of the Bull

Taurus is wealth. It is not just money, property, and the richness of material possessions, but also a wealth of the spirit. Taurus rules everything in the visible world we see, touch, hear, smell, taste—the Earth, sea, and sky—everything we normally consider "real." It is the sign of economy and reserve, for it is a mixture of thrift and luxury, generosity and practicality. It is a blend of the spiritual and material, for the fertility of the sign is unlimited, and in this sense it is the mystical bank of life. Yet it must hold the fruit of its efforts in its hands and seeks to realize its fantasy-rich imagination with tangible rewards.

Loyalty and endurance make this sign perhaps the most stable of all. We can lean on Taurus, count on it, and it makes our earthly lives comfortable, safe, pleasurable. It is warm, sensitive, loving, and capable of magnificent, joyful sensations. It is conservative and pragmatic, with a need to be sure of each step forward. It is the capacity to plan around eventualities without living in the future. Steadfast and constant, this is a sturdy combination of ruggedness and beauty, gentleness and unshakability of purpose. It is the point at which we join body and soul. Unselfish friend and loyal companion, Taurus is profoundly noble and openly humanitarian. Tenacity and concentration slow the energy down to bring certain long-lasting rewards.

Taurus is a fertile resource and rich ground to grow in, and we all need it for our ideas and plans to flourish. It is the uncut diamond, symbolizing rich, raw tastes and a deep need for satisfaction, refinement, and completion.

GEMINI
The Sign of the Twins

Gemini is the sign of mental brilliance. Communication is developed to a high degree of fluidity, rapidity, fluency. It is the chance for expressing ideas and relaying information from one place to another. Charming, debonair, and lighthearted, it is a symbol of universal interest and eternal curiosity. The mind is quick and advanced, with a lightning-like ability to assimilate data.

It is the successful manipulation of verbal or visual language and the capacity to meet all events with objectivity and intelligence. It is light, quick wit, with a comic satiric twist. Gemini is the sign of writing or speaking.

Gemini is the willingness to try anything once, a need to wander and explore, the quick shifting of moods and attitudes being a basic characteristic that indicates a need for change. Versatility is the remarkable Gemini attribute. It is the capacity to investigate, perform, and relate over great areas for short periods of time and thus to connect all areas. It is mastery of design and perception, the power to conceptualize and create by putting elements together—people, colors, patterns. It is the reporter's mind, plus a brilliant ability to see things in objective, colorful arrangement. Strength lies in constant refreshment of outlook and joyful participation in all aspects of life.

Gemini is involvement with neighbors, family and relatives, telephones, arteries of news and communication—anything that enhances the human capacity for communication and self-expression. It is active, positive, and energetic, with an insatiable hunger for human interchange. Through Gemini bright and dark sides of personality merge and the mind has wings. As it flies it reflects the light of a boundless shining intellect. It is the development of varied talents from recognition of the duality of self.

Gemini is geared toward enjoying life to the fullest by finding, above all else, a means of expressing the inner self to the outside world.

CANCER
The Sign of the Crab

Cancer is the special relationship to home and involvement with the family unit. Maintaining harmony in the domestic sphere or improving conditions there is a major characteristic in this sector of the Zodiac. Cancer is attachment between two beings vibrating in sympathy with one another.

It is the comfort of a loving embrace, a tender generosity. Cancer is the place of shelter whenever there are lost or hungry souls in the night. Through Cancer we are fed, protected, comforted, and soothed. When the coldness of the world threatens, Cancer is there with gentle understanding. It is protection and understated loyalty, a medium of rich, living feeling that is both psychic and mystical. Highly intuitive, Cancer has knowledge that other signs do not possess. It is the wisdom of the soul.

It prefers the quiet contentment of the home and hearth to the busy search for earthly success and civilized pleasures. Still, there is a respect for worldly knowledge. Celebration of life comes through food. The sign is the muted light of warmth, security, and gladness, and its presence means nourishment. It rules fertility and the instinct to populate and raise young. It is growth of the soul. It is the ebb and flow of all our tides of feeling, involvements, habits, and customs.

Through Cancer is reflected the inner condition of all human beings, and therein lies the seed of knowledge out of which the soul will grow.

LEO
The Sign of the Lion

Leo is love. It represents the warmth, strength, and regeneration we feel through love. It is the radiance of life-giving light and the center of all attention and activity. It is passion, romance, adventure, and games. Pleasure, amusement, fun, and entertainment are all part of

Leo. Based on the capacity for creative feeling and the desire to express love, Leo is the premier sign. It represents the unlimited outpouring of all that is warm and positive.

It is loyalty, dignity, responsibility, and command. Pride and nobility belong to Leo, and the dashing image of the knight in shining armor, of the hero, is part of Leo. It is a sense of high honor and kingly generosity born out of deep, noble love. It is the excitement of the sportsman, with all the unbeatable flair and style of success. It is a strong, unyielding will and true sense of personal justice, a respect for human freedom, and an enlightened awareness of people's needs.

Leo is involvement in the Self's awareness of personal talents and the desire and need to express them. At best it is forthrightness, courage and efficiency, authority and dignity, showmanship, and a talent for organization. Dependable and ardent, the Lion is characterized by individuality, positivism, and integrity.

It is the embodiment of human maturity, the effective individual in society, a virile creative force able to take chances and win. It is the love of laughter and the joy of making others happy. Decisive and enthusiastic, the Lion is the creative producer of the Zodiac It is the potential to light the way for others.

VIRGO
The Sign of the Virgin

Virgo is the sign of work and service. It is the symbol of the farmer at harvest time, and represents tireless efforts for the benefit of humanity, the joy of bringing the fruits of the Earth to the table of mankind. Celebration through work is the characteristic of this sign.

Sincerity, zeal, discipline, and devotion mark the sign of the Virgin.

The key word is purity, and in Virgo lies a potential for unlimited self-mastery. Virgo is the embodiment of perfected skill and refined talent. The thread of work is woven into the entire life of Virgo. All creativity is poured into streamlining a job, classifying a system, eradicating unnecessary elements of pure analysis. The true Virgo genius is found in separating the wheat from the chaff.

Spartan simplicity characterizes this sign, and Virgo battles the war between order and disorder. The need to arrange, assimilate, and categorize is great; it is the symbol of the diagnostician, the nurse, and the healer. Criticism and analysis describe this sign—pure, incisive wisdom and a shy appreciation of life's joys. All is devoted to the attainment of perfection and the ideal of self-mastery.

Virgo is the sign of health and represents the physical body as a functioning symbol of the mental and spiritual planes. It is the state of healing the ills of the human being with natural, temperate living. It is maturation of the ego as it passes from a self-centered phase to its awareness and devotion to humanity.

It is humanitarian, pragmatic, and scientific, with boundless curiosity. Focus and clarity of mind are the strong points, while strength of purpose and shy reserve underlie the whole sign. There is separateness, aloofness, and solitude for this beacon of the Zodiac. As a lighthouse guides ships, so Virgo shines.

LIBRA
The Sign of the Scales

Libra is the sign of human relationship, marriage, equality, and justice. It symbolizes the need of one human being for another, the capacity to find light, warmth, and life-giving love in relationship to another human being. It is union on any level—mental, sexual, emotional, or business. It is self-extension in a desire to find a partner with whom to share our joys. It is the capacity to recognize the needs of others and to develop to the fullest our powers of diplomacy, good taste, and refinement.

Libra is harmony, grace, aesthetic sensibility, and the personification of the spirit of companionship. It represents the skill to maintain balances and the ability to share mutually all life's benefits, trials, crises, and blessings. Libra is mastery at anticipation of another's needs or reactions. It is the exercise of simple justice with impartial delicacy.

It is the need to relate, to find a major person, place, or thing to sustain us and draw out our attention. It is growth through becoming awakened to the outside world and other people. It is the union of two loving souls in honesty, equality, mutual cooperation, and mutual accord.

SCORPIO
The Sign of the Scorpion

Scorpio is the sign of dark intensity, swirling passion, and sexual magnetism. It is the thirst for survival and regeneration that are the bases of sexual orientation and the creative impulses for self-expression. No other sign has such a profound instinct for survival and reproduction. Out of the abyss of emotions come a thousand creations, each one possessing a life of its own.

Scorpio is completion, determination, and endurance, fortified with enough stamina to outlive any enemy. It is the pursuit of goals despite any threat, warning, or obstacle that might stand in the way. It simply cannot be stopped. It knows when to wait and when to proceed. It is the constant state of readiness, a vibrant living force that constantly pumps out its rhythm from the depths of being.

Secretive and intimate, Scorpio symbolizes the self-directed creature with a will of steel. It is the flaming desire to create, manipulate, and control with a magician's touch. But the most mysterious quality is the capacity for metamorphosis, or total transformation.

This represents supremacy in the battle with dark unseen forces. It is the state of being totally fearless—the embodiment of truth and courage. It symbolizes the human capacity to face all danger and emerge supreme, to heal oneself. As a caterpillar spins its way into the darkness of a cocoon, Scorpio faces the end of existence, says goodbye to an old way of life, and goes through a kind of death—or total change.

Then, amid the dread of uncertainty, something remarkable happens. From hopelessness or personal crisis a new individual emerges, like a magnificent butterfly leaving behind its cocoon. It is a human being completely transformed and victorious. This is Scorpio.

SAGITTARIUS
The Sign of the Archer

Sagittarius is the sign of adventure and a thousand and one new experiences. It is the cause and purpose of every new attempt at adventure or self-understanding. It is the embodiment of enthusiasm, search for truth, and love of wisdom. Hope and optimism characterize this section of the Zodiac, and it is the ability to leave the past behind and set out again with positive resilience and a happy, cheerful outlook.

It is intelligence and exuberance, youthful idealism, and the desire to expand all horizons. It is the constant hatching of dreams, the hunger for knowledge, travel and experience. The goal is exploration itself.

Sagittarius is generosity, humor, and goodness of nature, backed up by the momentum of great expectations. It symbolizes the ability of people to be back in the race after having the most serious spills over the biggest hurdles. It is a healthy, positive outlook and the capacity to meet each new moment with unaffected buoyancy.

At this point in the Zodiac, greater conscious understanding begins to develop self-awareness and self-acceptance. It is an Olympian capacity to look upon the bright side and to evolve that aspect of mind we call conscience.

CAPRICORN
The Sign of the Sea Goat

Capricorn is the sign of structure and physical law. It rules depth, focus, and concentration. It is the symbol of success through perseverance, happiness through profundity. It is victory over disruption, and finds reality in codes set up by society and culture. It is the perpetuation of useful, tested patterns and a desire to protect what has already been established.

It is cautious, conservative, conscious of the passage of time, yet ageless. The Goat symbolizes the incorporation of reason into living and depth into loving. Stability, responsibility, and fruitfulness through loyalty color this sector of the Zodiac with an undeniable and irrepressible awareness of success, reputation, and honor. Capricorn is the culmination of our earthly dreams, the pinnacle of our worldly life.

It is introspection and enlightenment through serious contemplation of the Self and its position in the world. It is mastery of understanding and the realization of dreams.

Capricorn is a winter blossom, a born professional with an aim of harmony and justice, beauty, grace, and success. It is the well-constructed pyramid: perfect and beautiful, architecturally correct, mysteriously implacable, and hard to know. It is highly organized and built on precise foundations to last and last and last. It is practical, useful yet magnificent and dignified, signifying permanence and careful planning. Like a pyramid, Capricorn has thick impenetrable walls, complex passageways, and false corridors. Yet somewhere at the heart of this ordered structure is the spirit of a mighty ruler.

AQUARIUS
The Sign of the Water Bearer

Aquarius is the symbol of idealized free society. It is the herding instinct in man as a social animal. It is the collection of heterogeneous elements of human consciousness in coherent peaceful coexistence. Friendship, goodwill, and harmonious contact are Aquarius attributes. It is founded on the principle of individual freedom and the brotherly love and respect for the rights of all men and women on Earth.

It is strength of will and purpose, altruism, and love of human fellowship. It is the belief in spontaneity and free choice, in the openness to live in a spirit of harmony and cooperation—liberated from restriction, repression, and conventional codes of conduct. It is the brilliant capacity to assimilate information instantaneously at the last minute and translate that information into immediate creative action, and so the result is to live in unpredictability.

This is the progressive mind, the collective mind—groups of people getting together to celebrate life. Aquarius is the child of the future, the utopian working for the betterment of the human race. Funds, charities, seeking better cities and better living conditions for others, involvement in great forms of media or communication, science or research in the hope of joining mankind to his higher self—this is all Aquarius.

It is invention, genius, revolution, discovery—instantaneous breakthrough from limitations. It's a departure from convention, eccentricity, the unexpected development that changes the course of history. It is the discovery of people and all the arteries that join them together. Aquarius is adventure, curiosity, exotic and alien appeal. It pours the water of life and intelligence for all humanity to drink. It is humanism, community, and the element of surprise.

PISCES
The Sign of the Fishes

Pisces is faith—undistracted, patient, all-forgiving faith—and therein lies the Pisces capacity for discipline, endurance, and stamina.

It is imagination and other-worldliness, the condition

of living a foggy, uncertain realm of poetry, music, and fantasy. Passive and compassionate, this sector of the Zodiac symbolizes the belief in the inevitability of life. It represents the view of life that everything exists in waves, like the sea. All reality as we know it is a dream, a magic illusion that must ultimately be washed away. Tides pull this way and that, whirlpools and undercurrents sweep across the bottom of life's existence, but in Pisces there is total acceptance of all tides, all rhythms, all possibilities. It is the final resolution of all personal contradictions and all confusing paradoxes.

It is the search for truth and honesty, and the devotion to love, utterly and unquestionably. It is the desire to act with wisdom, kindness, and responsibility and to welcome humanity completely free from scorn, malice, discrimination, or prejudice. It is total, all-embracing, idealistic love. It is the acceptance of two sides of a question at once and love through sacrifice.

Pisces is beyond reality. We are here today, but may be gone tomorrow. Let the tide of circumstances carry you where it will, for nothing is forever. As all things come, so must they go. In the final reel, all things must pass away. It is deliverance from sorrow through surrender to the infinite. The emotions are as vast as the ocean, yet in the pain of confusion there is hope in the secret cell of one's own heart. Pisces symbolizes liberation from pain through love, faith, and forgiveness.

THE SIGNS AND
THEIR KEY WORDS

		Positive	Negative
ARIES	self	courage, initiative, pioneer instinct	brash rudeness, selfish impetuosity
TAURUS	money	endurance, loyalty, wealth	obstinacy, gluttony
GEMINI	mind	versatility, communication	capriciousness, unreliability
CANCER	family	sympathy, homing instinct	clannishness, childishness
LEO	children	love, authority, integrity	egotism, force
VIRGO	work	purity, industry, analysis	faultfinding, cynicism
LIBRA	marriage	harmony, justice	vacillation, superficiality
SCORPIO	sex	survival, regeneration	vengeance, discord
SAGITTARIUS	travel	optimism, higher learning	lawlessness, irresponsibility
CAPRICORN	career	depth, responsibility	narrowness, gloom
AQUARIUS	friends	humanity, genius	perverse unpredictability
PISCES	faith	spiritual love, universality	diffusion, escapism

THE ELEMENTS AND
THE QUALITIES OF THE SIGNS

Every sign has both an element and a quality associated with it. The element indicates the basic makeup of the sign, and the quality describes the kind of activity associated with each.

Element	Sign	Quality	Sign
Fire	Aries Leo Sagittarius	Cardinal	Aries Libra Cancer Capricorn
Earth	Taurus Virgo Capricorn	Fixed	Taurus Leo Scorpio Aquarius
Air	Gemini Libra Aquarius	Mutable	Gemini Virgo Sagittarius Pisces
Water	Cancer Scorpio Pisces		

•

Signs can be grouped together according to their element and quality. Signs of the same element share many basic traits in common. They tend to form stable configurations and ultimately harmonious relationships. Signs of the same quality are often less harmonious, but share many dynamic potentials for growth and profound fulfillment.

The following pages describe these sign groupings in more detail.

The Fire Signs

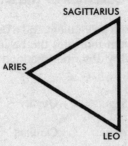

This is the fire group. On the whole these are emotional, volatile types, quick to anger, quick to forgive. They are adventurous, powerful people and act as a source of inspiration for everyone. They spark into action with immediate exuberant impulses. They are intelligent, self-involved, creative, and idealistic. They all share a certain vibrancy and glow that outwardly reflects an inner flame and passion for living.

The Earth Signs

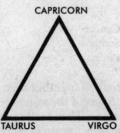

This is the earth group. They are in constant touch with the material world and tend to be conservative. Although they are all capable of spartan self-discipline, they are earthy, sensual people who are stimulated by the tangible, elegant, and luxurious. The thread of their lives is always practical, but they do fantasize and are often attracted to dark, mysterious, emotional people. They are like great cliffs overhanging the sea, forever married to the ocean but always resisting erosion from the dark, emotional forces that thunder at their feet.

The Air Signs

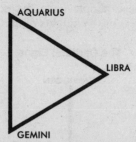

This is the air group. They are light, mental creatures desirous of contact, communication, and relationship. They are involved with people and the forming of ties on many levels. Original thinkers, they are the bearers of human news. Their language is their sense of word, color, style, and beauty. They provide an atmosphere suitable and pleasant for living. They add change and versatility to the scene, and it is through them that we can explore human intelligence and experience.

The Water Signs

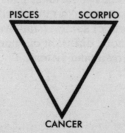

This is the water group. Through the water people, we are all joined together on emotional, nonverbal levels.

The water signs are silent, mysterious types whose magic hypnotizes even the most determined realist. They have uncanny perceptions about people and are as rich as the oceans when it comes to feeling, emotion, or imagination. They are sensitive, mystical creatures with memories that go back beyond time. Through water, life is sustained. These people have the potential for the depths of darkness or the heights of mysticism and art.

The Cardinal Signs .

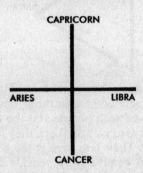

The cardinal signs present a picture of dynamism, activity, tremendous stress, and remarkable achievement. These people know the meaning of great change since their lives are often characterized by significant crises and major successes. The cardinal signs mark the beginning of the four seasons. And this combination is like a simultaneous storm of summer, fall, winter, and spring. The danger is chaotic diffusion of energy; the potential is irrepressible growth and victory.

The Fixed Signs

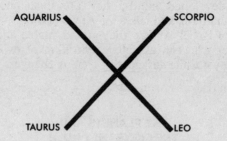

Fixed signs are always establishing themselves in a given place or area of experience. Like explorers who arrive and plant a flag, these people claim a position from which they do not enjoy being deposed. They are staunch, stalwart, upright, trusty, honorable people, although their obstinacy is well-known. Their contribution is fixity, and they are the angels who support our visible world.

The Mutable Signs

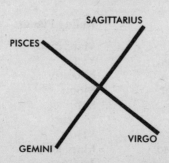

Mutable people are versatile, sensitive, intelligent, nervous, and deeply curious about life. They are the translators of all energy. They often carry out or complete tasks initiated by others. People from mutable signs have highly developed minds; they are imaginative and jumpy and think and talk a lot. At worst their lives are a Tower of Babel. At best they are adaptable and ready creatures who can assimilate one kind of experience and enjoy it while anticipating coming changes.

THE PLANETS AND
THE SIGNS THEY RULE

The signs of the Zodiac are linked to the planets in the following way. Each sign is governed or ruled by one or more planets. No matter where the planets are located in the sky at any given moment, they still rule their respective signs. When they travel through the signs they rule, they have special dignity and their effects are stronger.

Following is a list of the planets and the signs they rule. After you read the definitions of the planets from pages 88 to 96, see if you can determine how the planet ruling your Sun sign has affected your life.

Signs	Ruling Planets
Aries	Mars, Pluto
Taurus	Venus
Gemini	Mercury
Cancer	Moon
Leo	Sun
Virgo	Mercury
Libra	Venus
Scorpio	Mars, Pluto
Sagittarius	Jupiter
Capricorn	Saturn
Aquarius	Saturn, Uranus
Pisces	Jupiter, Neptune

THE ZODIAC AND
THE HUMAN BODY

The signs of the Zodiac are linked to the human body in a direct relationship. Each sign has a part of the body with which it is associated.

It is traditionally believed that surgery is best performed when the Moon is passing through a sign *other* than the sign associated with the part of the body upon which an operation is to be performed. But often the presence of the Moon in a particular sign will bring the focus of attention to that very part of the body under medical scrutiny.

The principles of medical astrology are complex and beyond the scope of this introduction. We can, however, list the signs of the Zodiac and the parts of the human body connected with them. Once you learn these correspondences, you'll be amazed at how accurate they are.

Signs	Human Body
Aries	Head, brain, face, upper jaw
Taurus	Throat, neck, lower jaw
Gemini	Hands, arms, lungs, nerves
Cancer	Stomach, breasts, womb, liver
Leo	Heart, spine
Virgo	Intestines, liver
Libra	Kidneys, lower back
Scorpio	Sex and eliminative organs
Sagittarius	Hips, thighs, liver
Capricorn	Skin, bones, teeth, knees
Aquarius	Circulatory system, lower legs
Pisces	Feet, tone of being

THE ZODIACAL HOUSES
AND THE RISING SIGN

Apart from the month and day of birth, the exact time of birth is another vital factor in the determination of an accurate horoscope. Not only do planets move with great speed, but one must know how far the Earth has turned during the day. That way you can determine exactly where the planets are located with respect to the precise birthplace of an individual. This makes your horoscope *your* horoscope.

The horoscope sets up a kind of framework around which the life of an individual grows like wild ivy, this way and that, weaving its way around the trellis of the natal positions of the planets. The year of birth tells us the positions of the distant, slow-moving planets Jupiter, Saturn, Uranus, Neptune, and Pluto. The month of birth indicates the Sun sign, or birth sign as it is commonly called, as well as indicating the positions of the rapidly moving planets Venus, Mercury, and Mars. The day of birth, as well as the time, locates the position of our Moon. And the moment of birth—the exact hour and minute—determines the houses through what is called the Ascendant, or Rising sign.

The illustration on the next page shows the flat chart, or natural wheel, an astrologer uses. The inner circle of the wheel is labeled 1 through 12. These 12 divisions are known as the houses of the Zodiac.

The 1st house always starts from the position marked E, which corresponds to the eastern horizon. The rest of the houses 2 through 12 follow around in a "counterclockwise" direction. The point where each house starts is known as a cusp, or edge.

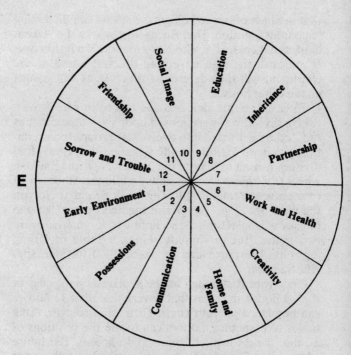

The 12 Houses of the Zodiac

The cusp, or edge, of the 1st house (point E) is where an astrologer would place your Rising sign, the Ascendant. The Rising sign is very important in a horoscope, as it defines your self-image, outlook, physical constitution, early environment, and whole orientation to life. And, as already mentioned, the exact time of your birth determines your Rising sign. Let's see how this works.

As the Earth rotates on its axis once every 24 hours, each one of the 12 signs of the Zodiac appears to be "rising" on the horizon, with a new one appearing about every two hours. Actually it is the turning of the Earth that exposes each sign to view, but you will remember that in much of our astrological work we are discussing "apparent" motion. This Rising sign marks the Ascendant, and it colors the whole orientation of a horoscope. It indicates the sign governing the first house of the chart, and will thus determine which signs will govern all the other houses.

To visualize this idea, imagine two color wheels with twelve divisions superimposed upon each other. Just as the Zodiac is divided into twelve star groups (constellations) that we identify as the signs, another twelvefold division is used to denote the houses. Now imagine one wheel (the signs) moving slowly while the other wheel (the houses) remains still. This analogy may help you see how the signs keep shifting the "color" of the houses as the Rising sign continues to change every two hours. But to simplify things, a Table of Rising Signs has been provided on pages 20–21 for your specific Sun sign.

Once your Rising sign has been placed on the cusp of the 1st house, the signs that govern the other 11 houses can be placed on your chart. Then an astrologer, using tables of planetary motion, can locate the positions of all the planets in their appropriate houses. The house where your Sun sign is describes your basic character and your fundamental drives. And the houses where the other planets are in your chart suggest the areas of life on Earth in which you will be most likely to focus your constant energy and center your activity.

The illustration on page 83 briefly identifies each of the•12 houses of the Zodiac. Now the pages that follow provide a detailed discussion of the meanings of the houses. In the section after the houses we will define all the known planets of the solar system, with a separate section on the Moon, in order to acquaint you with more of the astrological vocabulary you will be meeting again and again.

THE MEANING OF THE HOUSES

The twelve houses of every horoscope represent areas of life on Earth, or regions of worldly experience. Depending on which sign of the Zodiac was rising on the eastern horizon at the moment of birth, the activity of each house will be "colored" by the zodiacal sign on its cusp, or edge. In other words, the sign falling on the first house will determine what signs will fall on the rest of the houses.

1 The first house determines the basic orientation to all of life on Earth. It indicates the body type, face, head, and brain. It rules your self-image, or the way others see you because of the way you see your self. This is the Ascendant of the horoscope and is the focus of energies of your whole chart. It acts like a prism through which all of the planetary light passes and is reflected in your life. It colors your outlook and influences everything you do and see.

2 This is the house of finances. Here is your approach to money and materialism in general. It indicates where the best sources are for you to improve your financial condition and your earning power as a whole. It indicates chances for gain or loss. It describes your values, alliances, and assets.

3 This is the house of the day-to-day mind. Short trips, communication, and transportation are associated with this house. It deals with routines, brothers and sisters, relatives, neighbors, and the near environment at hand. Language, letters, and the tools for transmitting information are included in third-house matters.

4 This is the house that describes your home and home life, parents, and childhood in the sense of indicating the kind of roots you come from. It symbolizes your present home and domestic situation and reflects your need for privacy and retreat from the world, indicating, of course, what kind of scene you require.

5   Pleasure, love affairs, amusements, parties, creativity, children. This is the house of passion and courtship and of expressing your talents, whatever they are. It is related to the development of your personal life and the capacity to express feeling and enjoy romance.

6   This is the house of work. Here there are tasks to be accomplished and maladjustments to be corrected. It is the house of health as well, and describes some of the likely places where physical health difficulties may appear. It rules routines, regimen, necessary jobs as opposed to a chosen career, army, navy, police—people employed, co-workers, and those in service to others. It indicates the individual's ability to harvest the fruit of his own efforts.

7   This is the house of marriage, partnership, and unions. It represents the alter ego, all people other than yourself, open confrontation with the public. It describes your partner and the condition of partnership as you discern it. In short, it is your "take" on the world. It indicates your capacity to make the transition from courtship to marriage and specifically what you seek out in others.

8   This is the house of deep personal transition, sex as a form of mutual surrender and interchange between human beings. It is the release from tensions and the completion of the creative processes. The eighth house also has to do with taxes, inheritances, and the finances of others, as well as death as the ending of cycles and crises.

9   This is the house of the higher mind, philosophy, religion, and the expression of personal conscience through moral codes. It indicates political leanings, ethical views, and the capacity of the individual for a broader perspective and deeper understanding of himself in relation to society. It is through the ninth house that you make great strides in learning and travel to distant places and come to know yourself through study, dreams, and wide experience.

10 This is the house of career, honor, and prestige. It marks the culmination of worldly experience and indicates the highest point you can reach, what you look up to, and how high you can go in this lifetime. It describes your parents, employers, and how you view authority figures, the condition and direction of your profession, and your position in the community.

11 This is the house of friendships. It describes your social behavior, your views on humanity, and your hopes, aspirations, and wishes for an ideal life. It will indicate what kinds of groups, clubs, organizations, and friendships you tend to form and what you seek out in your chosen alliances other than with your mate or siblings. This house suggests the capacity for the freedom and unconventionality that an individual is seeking, his sense of his connection with mankind, and the definition of his goals, personal and social.

12 This is the house of seclusion, secret wisdom, and self-incarceration. It indicates our secret enemies as well, in the sense that there may be persons, feelings, or memories we are trying to escape. It is self-undoing in that this house acts against the ego in order to find a higher, more universal purpose. It rules prisons, hospitals, charities, and selfless service. It is the house of unfinished psychic business.

THE PLANETS OF THE SOLAR SYSTEM

The planets of the solar system all travel around the Sun at different speeds and different distances. Taken with the Sun, they all distribute individual intelligence and ability throughout the entire chart.

The planets modify the influence of the Sun in a chart according to their own particular natures, strengths, and positions. Their positions must be calculated for each year and day, and their function and expression in a horoscope will change as they move from one area of the Zodiac to another.

Following, you will find brief statements of their pure meanings.

THE SUN

The Sun is the center of existence. Around this flaming sphere all the planets revolve in endless orbits. Our star is constantly sending out its beams of light and energy without which no life on Earth would be possible. In astrology it symbolizes everything we are trying to become, the center around which all of our activity in life will always revolve. It is the symbol of our basic nature and describes the natural and constant thread that runs through everything that we do from birth to death on this planet.

Everything in the horoscope ultimately revolves around this singular body. Although other forces may be prominent in the charts of some individuals, still the Sun is the total nucleus of being and symbolizes the

THE SUN

complete potential of every human being alive. It is vitality and the life force. Your whole essence comes from the position of the Sun.

You are always trying to express the Sun according to its position by house and sign. Possibility for all development is found in the Sun, and it marks the fundamental character of your personal radiations all around you.

It symbolizes strength, vigor, ardor, generosity, and the ability to function effectively as a mature individual and a creative force in society. It is consciousness of the gift of life. The undeveloped solar nature is arrogant pushy, undependable, and proud, and is constantly using force.

MERCURY

Mercury is the planet closest to the Sun. It races around our star, gathering information and translating it to the rest of the system. Mercury represents your capacity to understand the desires of your own will and to translate those desires into action.

MERCURY

In other words it is the planet of mind and the power of communication. Through Mercury we develop an ability to think, write, speak, and observe—to become aware of the world around us. It colors our attitudes and vision of the world, as well as our capacity to communicate our inner responses to the outside world. Some people who have serious disabilities in their power of verbal communication have often wrongly been described as people lacking intelligence.

Although this planet (and its position in the horoscope) indicates your power to communicate your thoughts and perceptions to the world, intelligence is something deeper. Intelligence is distributed throughout all the planets. It is the relationship of the planets to each other that truly describes what we call intelligence. Mercury rules speaking, language, mathematics, draft and design, students, messengers, young people, offices, teachers, and any pursuits where the mind of man has wings.

VENUS

Venus is beauty. It symbolizes the harmony and radiance of a rare and elusive quality: beauty itself. It is refinement and delicacy, softness and charm. In astrology it indicates grace, balance, and the aesthetic sense. Where Venus is we see beauty, a gentle drawing in of energy and the need for satisfaction and completion. It is a special touch that finishes off rough edges.

VENUS

Venus is the planet of sensitivity and affection, and it is always the place for that other elusive phenomenon:

love. Venus describes our sense of what is beautiful and loving. Poorly developed, it is vulgar, tasteless, and self-indulgent. But its ideal is the flame of spiritual love— Aphrodite, goddess of love, and the sweetness and power of personal beauty.

MARS

Mars is raw, crude energy. The planet next to Earth but outward from the Sun is a fiery red sphere that charges through the horoscope with force and fury. It represents the way you reach out for new adventure and new experience. It is energy drive, initiative, courage, daring. It is the power to start something and see it through. It can be thoughtless, cruel and wild, angry and hostile, causing cuts, burns, scalds, wounds. It can stab its way through a chart, or it can be the symbol of healthy spirited adventure, well-channeled constructive power to begin and keep up the drive.

MARS

If you have trouble starting things, if you lack the get-up-and-go to start the ball rolling, if you lack aggressiveness and self-confidence, chances are there's another planet influencing your Mars. Mars rules soldiers, butchers, surgeons, salespeople—in general any field that requires daring, bold skill, operational technique, or self-promotion.

JUPITER

Jupiter is the largest planet of the solar system. Planet Jupiter rules good luck and good cheer, health, wealth, optimism, happiness, success, joy. It is the symbol of opportunity and always opens the way for new possibilities in your life. It rules exuberance, enthusiasm, wisdom, knowledge, generosity, and all forms of expansion in general. It rules actors, statesmen, clerics, professional people, religion, publishing, and the distribution of many people over large areas.

JUPITER

Sometimes Jupiter makes you think you deserve everything, and you become sloppy, wasteful, careless and rude, prodigal and lawless, in the illusion that nothing can ever go wrong. Then there is the danger of your showing overconfidence, exaggeration, undependability, and overindulgence.

Jupiter is the minimization of limitation and the emphasis on spirituality and potential. It is the thirst for knowledge and higher learning.

SATURN

Saturn circles our system in dark splendor with its mysterious rings, forcing us to be awakened to whatever we have neglected in the past. It will present real puzzles and problems to be solved, causing delays, obstacles, and hindrances. By doing so, Saturn stirs our own sensitivity to those areas where we are laziest.

SATURN

Here we must patiently develop method, and only through painstaking effort can our ends be achieved. It brings order to a horoscope and imposes reason just where we are feeling least reasonable. By creating limitations and boundary, Saturn shows the consequences of being human and demands that we accept the changing cycles inevitable in human life. Saturn rules time, old age, and sobriety. It can bring depression, gloom, jealousy, and greed, or serious acceptance of responsibilities out of which success will develop. With Saturn there is nothing to do but face facts. It rules laborers, stones, granite, rocks, and crystals.

THE OUTER PLANETS: URANUS, NEPTUNE, PLUTO

Uranus, Neptune, and Pluto are the outer planets. They liberate human beings from cultural conditioning, and in that sense are the lawbreakers. In early times it was thought that Saturn was the last planet of the solar system—the outer limit beyond which we could never go. The discovery of the next three planets beyond Saturn ushered in new phases of human history, revolution, and technology.

URANUS

Uranus rules unexpected change, upheaval, revolution. It is the symbol of total independence and asserts the freedom of an individual from all restriction and restraint. It is a breakthrough planet and indicates talent, originality, and genius in a horoscope. It usually causes last-minute reversals and changes of plan, unwanted separations, accidents, catastrophes, and eccentric behavior. It can add irrational rebelliousness and perverse bohemianism to a personality or a streak of unaffected brilliance in science and art.

URANUS

Uranus rules technology, aviation, and all forms of electrical and electronic advancement. It governs great leaps forward and topsy-turvy situations, and always turns things around at the last minute. Its effects are difficult to predict, since it rules sudden last-minute decisions and events that come like lightning out of the blue.

NEPTUNE

Neptune dissolves existing reality the way the sea erodes the cliffs beside it. Its effects are subtle like the ringing of a buoy's bell in the fog. It suggests a reality higher than definition can usually describe. It awakens a sense of higher responsibility often causing guilt, worry, anxieties, or delusions. Neptune is associated with all forms of escape and can make things seem a certain way so convincingly that you are absolutely sure of something that eventually turns out to be quite different.

NEPTUNE

It is the planet of illusion and therefore governs the invisible realms that lie beyond our ordinary minds, beyond our simple factual ability to prove what is "real." Treachery, deceit, disillusionment, and disappointment are linked to Neptune. It describes a vague reality that promises eternity and the divine, yet in a manner so complex that we cannot really fathom it at all. At its worst Neptune is a cheap intoxicant; at its best it is the poetry, music, and inspiration of the higher planes of spiritual love. It has dominion over movies, photographs, and much of the arts.

PLUTO

Pluto lies at the outpost of our system and therefore rules finality in a horoscope—the final closing of chapters in your life, the passing of major milestones and points of development from which there is no return. It is a final wipeout, a closeout, an evacuation. It is a subtle but powerful catalyst in all transformations that occur. It creates, destroys, then recreates. Sometimes Pluto starts its influence with a minor event or insignificant incident that might even go unnoticed. Slowly but surely, little by little, everything changes, until at last there has been a total transformation in the area of your life where Pluto has been operating. It rules mass thinking and the trends that society first rejects, then adopts, and finally outgrows.

PLUTO

Pluto rules the dead and the underworld—all the powerful forces of creation and destruction that go on all the time beneath, around, and above us. It can bring a lust for power with strong obsessions.

It is the planet that rules the metamorphosis of the caterpillar into a butterfly, for it symbolizes the capacity to change totally and forever a person's lifestyle, way of thought, and behavior.

THE MOON

Exactly how does the Moon affect us psychologically and psychically? We know it controls the tides. We understand how it affects blood rhythm and body tides, together with all the chemical fluids that constitute our physical selves. Astronauts have walked upon its surface, and our scientists are now studying and analyzing data that will help determine the age of our satellite, its origin, and makeup.

THE MOON

But the true mystery of that small body as it circles our Earth each month remains hidden. Is it really a dead, lifeless body that has no light or heat of its own, reflecting only what the gigantic Sun throws toward it? Is it a sensitive reflecting device, which translates the blinding, billowing energy from our star into a language our bodies can understand?

In astrology, the Moon is said to rule our feelings, customs, habits, and moods. As the Sun is the constant, ever shining source of life in daytime, the Moon is our nighttime mother, lighting up the night and swiftly moving, reflecting ever so rapidly the changing phases of behavior and personality. If we feel happy or joyous, or we notice certain habits and repetitive feelings that bubble up from our dark centers then vanish as quickly as they appeared, very often it is the position of the Moon that describes these changes.

THE MOON IN ALL SIGNS

The Moon moves quickly through the Zodiac, that is, through all twelve signs of our Sun's apparent path. It stays in each sign for about 2¼ days. During its brief stay in a given sign, the moods and responses of people are always colored by the nature of that sign, any planets located there at that time, or any other heavenly bodies placed in such a way that the Moon will pick up their "vibration" as well. It's astonishing to observe how clearly the Moon changes people's interests and involvements as it moves along.

The following section gives brief descriptions of the Moon's influence in each sign.

MOON IN ARIES

There's excitement in the air. Some new little thing appears, and people are quick and full of energy and enterprise, ready for something new and turning on to a new experience. There's not much patience or hesitation, doubt or preoccupation with guilty self-damning recriminations. What's needed is action. People feel like putting their plans into operation. Pleasure and adventure characterize the mood, and it's time for things to change, pick up, improve. Confidence, optimism, positive feeling pervade the air. Sick people take a turn for the better. Life stirs with a feeling of renewal. People react bravely to challenges, with a sense of courage and dynamism. Self-reliance is the key word, and people minimize their problems and maximize the power to exercise freedom of the will. There is an air of abruptness and shortness of consideration, as people are feeling the courage of their convictions to do something for themselves. Feelings are strong and intuitive, and the mood is idealistic and freedom-oriented.

MOON IN TAURUS

Here the mood is just as pleasure loving, but less idealistic. Now the concerns are more materialistic, money-oriented, down-to-earth. The mood is stable, diligent, thoughtful, deliberate. It is a time when feelings are rich and deep, with a profound appreciation of the good things the world has to offer and the pleasures of the sensations. It is a period when people's minds are serious, realistic, and devoted to the increases and improvements of property and possessions and acquisition of wealth. There is a conservative tone, and people are fixed in their views, needing to add to their stability in every way. Assessment of assets, criticism, and the execution of tasks are strong involvements of the Taurus Moon when financial matters demand attention. It is devotion to security on a financial and emotional level. It is a fertile time, when ideas can begin to take root and grow.

MOON IN GEMINI

There is a rapid increase in movement. People are going places, exchanging ideas and information. Gossip and news travel fast under a Gemini Moon, because people are naturally involved with communication, finding out things from some, passing on information to others. Feelings shift to a mental level now, and people feel and say things that are sincere at the moment but lack the root and depth to endure much beyond the moment. People are involved with short-term engagements, quick trips. There is a definite need for changing the scene. You'll find people flirtatious and talkative, experimental and easygoing, falling into encounters they hadn't planned on. The mind is quick and active, with powers of writing and speaking greatly enhanced. Radio, television, letters, newspapers, magazines are in the spotlight with the Moon in Gemini, and new chances pop up for self-expression, with new people involved. Relatives and neighbors are tuned in to you and you to them. Take advantage of this fluidity of mind. It can rescue you from worldly involvements and get you into new surroundings for a short while.

MOON IN CANCER

Now you'll see people heading home. People turn their attention inward to their place of residence under a Cancer Moon. The active, changeable moods of yesterday vanish, and people settle in as if they were searching for a nest of security. Actually people are retiring, seeking to find peace and quiet within themselves. That's what they're feeling when they prefer to stay home rather than go out with a crowd of people to strange places. They need the warmth and comfort of the family and hearth. Maybe they feel anxious and insecure from the hustle and bustle of the workaday world. Maybe they're just tired. But it's definitely a time of tender need for emotional sustenance. It's a time for nostalgia and returning to times and places that once nourished deeply. Thoughts of parents, family, and old associations come to people. The heritage of their family ties holds them strongly now. These are personal needs that must be fed. Moods are deep and mysterious and sometimes sad. People are silent, psychic, and imaginative during this period. It's a fruitful time when people respond to love, food, and all the comforts of the inner world.

MOON IN LEO

The shift is back out in the world, and people are born again, like kids. They feel zestful, passionate, exuberant and need plenty of attention. They're interested in having a good time, enjoying themselves, and the world of entertainment takes over for a while. Places of amusement, theaters, parties, sprees, a whole gala of glamorous events, characterize this stage of the Moon's travel. Gracious, lavish hosting and a general feeling of buoyancy and flamboyance are in the air. It's a time of sunny, youthful fun when people are in the mood to take chances and win. The approach is direct, ardent, and strong. Bossy, authoritarian feelings predominate, and people throw themselves forward for all they're worth. Flattery is rampant, but the ego is vibrant and flourishing with the kiss of life, romance, and love. Speculation is indicated, and it's usually a time to go out and try your hand at love. Life is full and rich as a summer meadow, and feelings are warm.

MOON IN VIRGO

The party's over. Eyelashes are on the table. This is a time for cleaning up after the merrymakers have gone home. People are now concerned with sobering up and getting personal affairs straight, clearing up any confusions or undefined feelings from the night before, and generally attending to the practical business of doctoring up after the party. People are back at work, concerned with necessary, perhaps tedious tasks—paying bills, fixing and adjusting things, and generally purifying their lives, streamlining their affairs, and involving themselves with work and service to the community. Purity is the key word in personal habits, diet, and emotional needs. Propriety and coolness take the place of yesterday's devil-may-care passion, and the results are a detached, inhibited period under a Virgo Moon.

Feelings are not omitted; they are merely subjected to the scrutiny of the mind and thus purified. Health comes to the fore, and people are interested in clearing up problems.

MOON IN LIBRA

Here there is a mood of harmony, when people strive to join with other people in a bond of peace and justice. At this time people need relationships and often seek the company of others in a smooth-flowing feeling of love, beauty, and togetherness. People make efforts to understand other people, and though it's not the best time to make decisions, many situations keep presenting themselves from the outside to change plans and offer new opportunities. There is a general search for accord between partners, and differences are explored as similarities are shared. The tone is concilatory, and the mood is one of cooperation, patience, and tolerance. People do not generally feel independent, and sometimes this need to share or lean on others disturbs them. It shouldn't. This is the moment for uniting and sharing, for feeling a mutual flow of kindness and tenderness between people. The air is ingratiating and sometimes lacks stamina, courage, and a consistent, definite point of view. But it is a time favoring the condition of beauty and the development of all forms of art.

MOON IN SCORPIO

This is not a mood of sharing. It's driving, intense, brooding—full of passion and desire. Its baser aspects are the impulses of selfishness, cruelty, and the pursuit of animal drives and appetites. There is a craving for excitement and a desire to battle and win in a bloodthirsty war for survival. It is competitive and ruthless, sarcastic and easily bruised, highly sexual and touchy, without being especially tender. Retaliation, jealousy, and revenge can be felt too during this time. Financial involvements, debts, and property issues arise now. Powerful underworld forces are at work here, and great care is needed to transform ignorance into wisdom, to keep the mind from descending into the lower depths. During the Moon's stay in Scorpio we contact the dark undercurrents swirling around and get in touch with a magical part of our natures. Interest lies in death, inheritance, and the powers of rebirth and regeneration.

MOON IN SAGITTARIUS

Here the mind climbs out of the depths, and people are involved with the higher, more enlightened, and conscious facets of their personality. There's a renewed interest in learning, education, and philosophy, and a new involvement with ethics, morals, national and international issues: a concern with looking for a better way to live. It's a time of general improvement, with people feeling more deeply hopeful and optimistic. They are dreaming of new places, new possibilities, new horizons. They are emerging from the abyss and leaving the past behind, with their eyes gazing toward the new horizon. They decide to travel, or renew their contacts with those far away. They question their religious beliefs and investigate new areas of metaphysical inquiry. It's a time for adventure, sports, playing the field—people have their eye on new possibilities. They are bored with depression and details. They feel restless and optimistic, joyous and delighted to be alive. Thoughts revolve around adventure, travel, liberation.

MOON IN CAPRICORN

When the Moon moves into Capricorn, things slow down considerably. People require a quiet, organized, and regularized condition. Their minds are sober and realistic, and they are methodically going about bringing their dreams and plans into reality. They are more conscious of what is standing between them and success, and during this time they take definite, decisive steps to remove any obstacles from their path. They are cautious, suspicious, sometimes depressed, discouraged, and gloomy, but they are more determined than ever to accomplish their tasks. They take care of responsibilities now, wake up to facts, and wrestle with problems and dilemmas of this world. They are politically minded and concerned with social convention now, and it is under a Capricorn Moon that conditioning and conformity elicit the greatest responses. People are moderate and serious and surround themselves with what is most familiar. They want predictable situations and need time to think deeply and deliberately about all issues. It's a time for planning.

MOON IN AQUARIUS

Spontaneity replaces the sober predictability of yesterday. Now events, people, and situations pop up, and you take advantage of unsought opportunities and can expect the unexpected. Surprises, reversals, and shifts in plans mark this period. There is a resurgence of optimism, and things you wouldn't expect to happen suddenly do. What you were absolutely sure was going to happen simply doesn't. Here there is a need for adventure born from a healthy curiosity that characterizes people's moods. Unrealistic utopias are dreamed of, and it is from such idealistic dreams that worlds of the future are built. There is a renewed interest in friendship, comradeship, community, and union on high planes of mental and spiritual companionship. People free each other from grudges or long-standing dead-locks, and there is a hopeful joining of hands in a spirit of love and peace. People don't feel like sticking to previous plans, and they must be able to respond to new situations at the last minute. People need freedom. Groups of people come together and meet, perhaps for a common purpose of having dinner or hearing music, and leave knowing each other better.

MOON IN PISCES

Flashes of brilliant insight and mysterious knowledge characterize the Moon's passage in Pisces. Sometimes valuable "truths" seem to emerge which, later in the light of day, turn out to be false. This is a time of poetry, intuition, and music, when worldly realities can be the most illusory and unreliable of all. There are often feelings of remorse, guilt, or sorrow connected with a Pisces Moon—sorrow from the childhood or family or past. Confusion, anxiety, worry, and a host of imagined pains and sorrows may drag you down until you cannot move or think. Often there are connections with hospitals, prisons, alcohol, drugs, and lower forms of escape. It is a highly emotional time, when the feelings and compassion for humanity and all people everywhere rise to the surface of your being. Mysteries of society and the soul now rise to demand solutions, but often the riddles posed during this period have many answers that all seem right. It is more a time for inner reflection than positive action. It is a time when poetry and music float to the surface of the being, and for the creative artist it is the richest source of inspiration.

MOON TABLES

CORRECTION FOR NEW YORK TIME, FIVE HOURS WEST OF GREENWICH

Atlanta, Boston, Detroit, Miami, Washington, Montreal,
Ottawa, Quebec, Bogota,
Havana, Lima, Santiago . . . . Same time

Chicago, New Orleans, Houston, Winnipeg, Churchill,
Mexico City. . . . . Deduct 1 hour

Albuquerque, Denver, Phoenix, El Paso, Edmonton,
Helena . . . . Deduct 2 hours

Los Angeles, San Francisco, Reno, Portland,
Seattle, Vancouver . . . . Deduct 3 hours

Honolulu, Anchorage, Fairbanks, Kodiak . . . . Deduct 5 hours

Nome, Samoa, Tonga, Midway . . . . Deduct 6 hours

Halifax, Bermuda, San Juan, Caracas, La Paz,
Barbados . . . . Add 1 hour

St. John's, Brasilia, Rio de Janeiro, Sao Paulo,
Buenos Aires, Montevideo . . . . Add 2 hours

Azores, Cape Verde Islands . . . . Add 3 hours

Canary Islands, Madeira, Reykjavik . . . . Add 4 hours

London, Paris, Amsterdam, Madrid, Lisbon,
Gibraltar, Belfast, Rabat. . . . . Add 5 hours

Frankfurt, Rome, Oslo, Stockholm, Prague,
Belgrade . . . . Add 6 hours

Bucharest, Beirut, Tel Aviv, Athens, Istanbul, Cairo,
Alexandria, Cape Town, Johannesburg. . . . . . . Add 7 hours

Moscow, Leningrad, Baghdad, Dhahran,
Addis Ababa, Nairobi, Teheran, Zanzibar . . . . Add 8 hours

Bombay, Calcutta, Sri Lanka. . . . . Add 10½ hours

Hong Kong, Shanghai, Manila, Peking,
Perth . . . . Add 13 hours

Tokyo, Okinawa, Darwin, Pusan . . . . Add 14 hours

Sydney, Melbourne, Port Moresby, Guam. . . . . . Add 15 hours

Auckland, Wellington, Suva, Wake . . . . Add 17 hours

2007 MOON SIGN DATES—NEW YORK TIME

JANUARY			FEBRUARY			MARCH		
Day Moon Enters			**Day Moon Enters**			**Day Moon Enters**		
1.	Gemini		1.	Leo	12:16 am	1.	Leo	
2.	Cancer	10:15 am	2.	Leo		2.	Virgo	4:33 pm
3.	Cancer		3.	Virgo	9:35 am	3.	Virgo	
4.	Leo	5:15 pm	4.	Virgo		4.	Virgo	
5.	Leo		5.	Libra	9:16 pm	5.	Libra	4:26 am
6.	Leo		6.	Libra		6.	Libra	
7.	Virgo	1:19 am	7.	Libra		7.	Scorp.	5:18 pm
8.	Virgo		8.	Scorp.	10:11 am	8.	Scorp.	
9.	Libra	1:16 pm	9.	Scorp.		9.	Scorp.	
10.	Libra		10.	Sagitt.	10:02 pm	10.	Sagitt.	5:36 am
11.	Libra		11.	Sagitt.		11.	Sagitt.	
12.	Scorp.	2:09 am	12.	Sagitt.		12.	Capric.	3:36 pm
13.	Scorp.		13.	Capric.	6:43 am	13.	Capric.	
14.	Sagitt.	1:12 pm	14.	Capric.		14.	Aquar.	9:53 pm
15.	Sagitt.		15.	Aquar.	11:36 am	15.	Aquar.	
16.	Capric.	8:50 pm	16.	Aquar.		16.	Aquar.	
17.	Capric.		17.	Pisces	1:31 pm	17.	Pisces	12:31 am
18.	Capric.		18.	Pisces		18.	Pisces	
19.	Aquar.	1:17 am	19.	Aries	2:07 pm	19.	Aries	12:43 am
20.	Aquar.		20.	Aries		20.	Aries	
21.	Pisces	3:49 am	21.	Taurus	3:04 pm	21.	Taurus	12:16 am
22.	Pisces		22.	Taurus		22.	Taurus	
23.	Aries	5:53 am	23.	Gemini	5:43 pm	23.	Gemini	1:07 am
24.	Aries		24.	Gemini		24.	Gemini	
25.	Taurus	8:30 am	25.	Cancer	10:49 pm	25.	Cancer	4:50 am
26.	Taurus		26.	Cancer		26.	Cancer	
27.	Gemini	12:11 pm	27.	Cancer		27.	Leo	12:05 pm
28.	Gemini		28.	Leo	6:31 am	28.	Leo	
29.	Cancer	5:17 pm				29.	Virgo	10:28 pm
30.	Cancer					30.	Virgo	
31.	Cancer					31.	Virgo	

Daylight saving time to be considered where applicable.

2007 MOON SIGN DATES—NEW YORK TIME

APRIL		MAY		JUNE	
Day Moon Enters		**Day Moon Enters**		**Day Moon Enters**	
1. Libra	10:44 am	1. Scorp.	5:42 am	1. Sagitt.	
2. Libra		2. Scorp.		2. Capric.	10:10 am
3. Scorp.	11:37 pm	3. Sagitt.	5:49 pm	3. Capric.	
4. Scorp.		4. Sagitt.		4. Aquar.	6:16 pm
5. Scorp.		5. Sagitt.		5. Aquar.	
6. Sagitt.	11:58 am	6. Capric.	4:22 am	6. Aquar.	
7. Sagitt.		7. Capric.		7. Pisces	12:25 am
8. Capric.	10:37 pm	8. Aquar.	12:49 pm	8. Pisces	
9. Capric.		9. Aquar.		9. Aries	4:27 am
10. Capric.		10. Pisces	6:33 pm	10. Aries	
11. Aquar.	6:24 am	11. Pisces		11. Taurus	6:30 am
12. Aquar.		12. Aries	9:20 pm	12. Taurus	
13. Pisces	10:40 am	13. Aries		13. Gemini	7:25 am
14. Pisces		14. Taurus	9:49 pm	14. Gemini	
15. Aries	11:48 am	15. Taurus		15. Cancer	8:46 am
16. Aries		16. Gemini	9:35 pm	16. Cancer	
17. Taurus	11:12 am	17. Gemini		17. Leo	12:26 pm
18. Taurus		18. Cancer	10:39 pm	18. Leo	
19. Gemini	10:52 am	19. Cancer		19. Virgo	7:47 pm
20. Gemini		20. Cancer		20. Virgo	
21. Cancer	12:51 pm	21. Leo	2:58 am	21. Virgo	
22. Cancer		22. Leo		22. Libra	5:45 am
23. Leo	6:39 pm	23. Virgo	11:27 am	23. Libra	
24. Leo		24. Virgo		24. Scorp.	7:26 pm
25. Leo		25. Libra	11:17 pm	25. Scorp.	
26. Virgo	4:25 am	26. Libra		26. Scorp.	
27. Virgo		27. Libra		27. Sagitt.	7:25 am
28. Libra	4:46 pm	28. Scorp.	12:12 pm	28. Sagitt.	
29. Libra		29. Scorp.		29. Capric.	5:06 pm
30. Libra		30. Scorp.		30. Capric.	
		31. Sagitt.	12:06 am		

Daylight saving time to be considered where applicable.

2007 MOON SIGN DATES—NEW YORK TIME

JULY		AUGUST		SEPTEMBER	
Day Moon Enters		**Day Moon Enters**		**Day Moon Enters**	
1. Capric.		1. Pisces		1. Taurus	12:36 am
2. Aquar.	12:25 am	2. Aries	3:44 pm	2. Taurus	
3. Aquar.		3. Aries		3. Gemini	2:31 am
4. Pisces	5:53 am	4. Taurus	6:17 pm	4. Gemini	
5. Pisces		5. Taurus		5. Cancer	6:09 am
6. Aries	9:58 am	6. Gemini	9:02 pm	6. Cancer	
7. Aries		7. Gemini		7. Leo	12:00 pm
8. Taurus	12:55 pm	8. Gemini		8. Leo	
9. Taurus		9. Cancer	12:37 am	9. Virgo	8:11 pm
10. Gemini	3:11 pm	10. Cancer		10. Virgo	
11. Gemini		11. Leo	5:43 am	11. Virgo	
12. Cancer	5:40 pm	12. Leo		12. Libra	6:32 am
13. Cancer		13. Virgo	1:04 pm	13. Libra	
14. Leo	9:44 pm	14. Virgo		14. Scorp.	6:38 pm
15. Leo		15. Libra	11:05 pm	15. Scorp.	
16. Leo		16. Libra		16. Scorp.	
17. Virgo	4:40 am	17. Libra		17. Sagitt.	7:22 am
18. Virgo		18. Scorp.	11:14 am	18. Sagitt.	
19. Libra	2:54 pm	19. Scorp.		19. Capric.	6:53 pm
20. Libra		20. Sagitt.	11:45 pm	20. Capric.	
21. Libra		21. Sagitt.		21. Capric.	
22. Scorp.	3:19 am	22. Sagitt.		22. Aquar.	3:19 am
23. Scorp.		23. Capric.	10:21 am	23. Aquar.	
24. Sagitt.	3:31 pm	24. Capric.		24. Pisces	7:56 am
25. Sagitt.		25. Aquar.	5:36 pm	25. Pisces	
26. Sagitt.		26. Aquar.		26. Aries	9:24 am
27. Capric.	1:22 am	27. Pisces	9:35 pm	27. Aries	
28. Capric.		28. Pisces		28. Taurus	9:18 am
29. Aquar.	8:15 am	29. Aries	11:26 pm	29. Taurus	
30. Aquar.		30. Aries		30. Gemini	9:35 am
31. Pisces	12:42 pm	31. Aries			

Daylight saving time to be considered where applicable.

2007 MOON SIGN DATES—NEW YORK TIME

OCTOBER			NOVEMBER			DECEMBER		
Day	**Moon Enters**		**Day**	**Moon Enters**		**Day**	**Moon Enters**	
1.	Gemini		1.	Leo		1.	Virgo	
2.	Cancer	11:58 am	2.	Leo		2.	Virgo	
3.	Cancer		3.	Virgo	7:46 am	3.	Libra	1:02 am
4.	Leo	5:26 pm	4.	Virgo		4.	Libra	
5.	Leo		5.	Libra	6:48 pm	5.	Scorp.	1:32 pm
6.	Leo		6.	Libra		6.	Scorp.	
7.	Virgo	2:04 am	7.	Libra		7.	Scorp.	
8.	Virgo		8.	Scorp.	7:19 am	8.	Sagitt.	2:12 am
9.	Libra	12:59 pm	9.	Scorp.		9.	Sagitt.	
10.	Libra		10.	Sagitt.	8:00 pm	10.	Capric.	1:52 pm
11.	Libra		11.	Sagitt.		11.	Capric.	
12.	Scorp.	1:14 am	12.	Sagitt.		12.	Capric.	
13.	Scorp.		13.	Capric.	8:02 am	13.	Aquar.	12:02 am
14.	Sagitt.	1:59 pm	14.	Capric.		14.	Aquar.	
15.	Sagitt.		15.	Aquar.	6:31 pm	15.	Pisces	8:16 am
16.	Sagitt.		16.	Aquar.		16.	Pisces	
17.	Capric.	2:04 am	17.	Aquar.		17.	Aries	1:54 pm
18.	Capric.		18.	Pisces	2:16 am	18.	Aries	
19.	Aquar.	11:52 am	19.	Pisces		19.	Taurus	4:39 pm
20.	Aquar.		20.	Aries	6:25 am	20.	Taurus	
21.	Pisces	6:03 pm	21.	Aries		21.	Gemini	5:15 pm
22.	Pisces		22.	Taurus	7:20 am	22.	Gemini	
23.	Aries	8:25 pm	23.	Taurus		23.	Cancer	5:19 pm
24.	Aries		24.	Gemini	6:30 am	24.	Cancer	
25.	Taurus	8:06 pm	25.	Gemini		25.	Leo	6:53 pm
26.	Taurus		26.	Cancer	6:08 am	26.	Leo	
27.	Gemini	7:12 pm	27.	Cancer		27.	Virgo	11:45 pm
28.	Gemini		28.	Leo	8:24 am	28.	Virgo	
29.	Cancer	7:51 pm	29.	Leo		29.	Virgo	
30.	Cancer		30.	Virgo	2:45 pm	30.	Libra	8:38 am
31.	Leo	11:49 pm				31.	Libra	

Daylight saving time to be considered where applicable.

2007 FISHING GUIDE

	Good	Best
January	1-5-6-19-25	2-3-4-11-30-31
February	1-2-3-4-17-24-28	16-26-27
March	1-2-3-4-11-18-30-31	5-6-25-26
April	17-24-29	2-3-4-5-9-29-30
May	4-5-10-24-31	1-2-15-29-30
June	1-2-14-28-29	3-4-8-23-26-30
July	2-3-7-27-29-30-31	13-23-28
August	2-12-20-26-27-30-31	1-5-24-28-29
September	4-11-22-23-26-27-28	20-24-25-29
October	18-24-25-28-29	3-10-22-26-27
November	2-17-21-22-24-25	9-23-26-27
December	1-10-17-21-22-23-26-27	24-25-31

2007 PLANTING GUIDE

	Aboveground Crops	Root Crops
January	3-21-22-26-30-31	3-10-11-12-13-17-18
February	18-22-23-26-27	6-7-8-9-14
March	21-22-25-26	5-6-7-8-9-13-14-18
April	1-18-22-23-29-30	2-3-4-5-9-10-14
May	1-19-20-26-27-28-29-30	1-2-11-12-15-16
June	15-16-22-23-24-25-26	3-4-7-8-11-12-30
July	20-21-22-23-28	3-4-9-12-14
August	16-17-18-19-24-25	1-5-6-10-28-29
September	12-13-14-15-16-20-21-25	2-5-6-29
October	12-13-18-22-23	3-10-26-27-30-31
November	14-15-18-19-22-23	7-8-9-26-27
December	11-12-16-20	4-5-6-7-24-25-30

	Pruning	Weeds and Pests
January	3-12-13	6-7-8-15-16
February	9-10	2-3-4-11-16
March	8-17-18	4-10-11-15-16
April	4-5-14	7-8-12-16
May	2-11-12	4-5-9-13-14
June	7-8	5-6-9-10-14
July	4-5-13-14	2-3-7-11-12-30
August	10-29	3-7-8-12-30-31
September	5-6	3-4-8-9-10-11-27
October	2-3-30-31	1-5-6-7-8-28-29
November	9-26-27	1-2-3-4-25-29-30
December	6-7-24-25	1-2-9-26-27-28-29

2007 PHASES OF THE MOON—
NEW YORK TIME

New Moon	First Quarter	Full Moon	Last Quarter
Dec. 20 ('06)	Dec. 27 ('06)	Jan. 3	Jan. 11
Jan. 18	Jan. 25	Feb. 2	Feb. 10
Feb. 17	Feb. 24	March 3	March 11
March 18	March 25	April 2	April 10
April 17	April 24	May 2	May 9
May 16	May 23	May 31	June 8
June 14	June 22	June 30	July 7
July 14	July 22	July 29	August 5
August 12	August 20	August 28	Sept. 3
Sept. 11	Sept. 19	Sept. 26	Oct. 3
Oct. 11	Oct. 19	Oct. 26	Nov. 1
Nov. 9	Nov. 17	Nov. 24	Dec. 1
Dec. 9	Dec. 17	Dec. 23	Dec. 31

Each phase of the Moon lasts approximately seven to eight days, during which the Moon's shape gradually changes as it comes out of one phase and goes into the next.

There will be a solar eclipse during the New Moon phase on March 18 and September 11.

There will be a lunar eclipse during the Full Moon phase on March 3 and August 28.

Use the Moon phases to connect you with your lucky numbers for this year. See the next page (page 112) and your lucky numbers.

LUCKY NUMBERS
FOR ARIES: 2007

Lucky numbers and astrology can be linked through the movements of the Moon. Each phase of the thirteen Moon cycles vibrates with a sequence of numbers for your Sign of the Zodiac over the course of the year. Using your lucky numbers is a fun system that connects you with tradition.

New Moon	First Quarter	Full Moon	Last Quarter
Dec. 20 ('06)	Dec. 27 ('06)	Jan. 3	Jan. 11
8 5 1 5	8 8 6 4	5 4 9 2	2 3 7 4
Jan. 18	Jan. 25	Feb. 2	Feb. 10
4 0 1 4	4 2 2 9	4 5 7 8	8 3 9 6
Feb. 17	Feb. 24	March 3	March 11
6 0 7 5	5 3 3 8	1 0 2 6	6 3 9 4
March 18	March 25	April 2	April 10
4 7 5 7	5 5 1 3	3 0 8 5	5 2 6 0
April 17	April 24	May 2	May 9
0 9 7 2	1 7 9 0	4 5 2 8	8 3 6 4
May 16	May 23	May 31	June 8
4 2 0 1	1 8 9 4	8 0 7 2	2 5 3 3
June 14	June 22	June 30	July 7
3 0 9 6	8 5 6 1	5 4 8 9	2 9 9 7
July 14	July 22	July 29	August 5
7 6 3 5	6 1 9 6	2 7 0 8	8 8 6 5
August 12	August 20	August 28	Sept. 3
6 2 4 5	5 9 0 7	6 9 5 3	3 0 9 6
Sept. 11	Sept. 19	Sept. 26	Oct. 3
8 9 4 4	1 7 3 0	9 9 4 4	2 1 7 9
Oct. 11	Oct. 19	Oct. 26	Nov. 1
9 1 5 2	2 8 3 0	7 7 5 4	5 1 3 4
Nov. 9	Nov. 17	Nov. 24	Dec. 1
4 8 5 2	6 9 7 1	7 8 7 4	4 6 7 2
Dec. 9	Dec. 17	Dec. 23	Dec. 31
2 8 5 9	9 3 1 6	5 3 9 2	8 3 7 4

ARIES
YEARLY FORECAST: 2007

Forecast for 2007 Concerning Business
Prospects, Financial Affairs, Health,
Travel, Employment, Love and Marriage
for Persons Born with the Sun
in the Zodiacal Sign of Aries,
March 21–April 20.

For those born under the influence of the Sun in the zodiacal sign of Aries, ruled by Mars, the planet of passion
and drive, this is a year for action, adventure, and excitement. The chance to spread your wings, to explore and
experience freedom awaits you. Your ruler Mars, along
with Jupiter and Pluto, begins the year in Sagittarius in
your solar ninth house of long journeys, philosophical
beliefs, knowledge, and wisdom. Travel may figure
prominently. The temptation to pack your bags and take
off for distant shores will be strong enough that you can
confidently expect to be moving around more both at
home and abroad.

Overseas journeys are likely to combine personal adventure with business and career matters. Travels of the
mind are also supported through higher education, philosophy, self-employment training, and skills-for-life
courses. All such study will increase knowledge and self-
confidence. Planning interesting itineraries, researching
exotic destinations, even organizing the mundane tasks
of applying for passports and visas will generate excitement. Long-distance travel is favored most of 2007. Va-
cations in the beginning of the year will be enjoyable if

you allow for intense situations in mid-January. This is a period when Aries travelers need to take extra safety precautions to avoid accidents. May and September are also times to be alert to possible danger.

For the employed and self-employed Aries, unexpected opportunities, travel, and study all play an important role in your working life. Employment prospects may prompt you to consider relocating to another state or country. Relocation may be necessary to further studies that will improve your education level and career prospects. Changing your residence, even your country of residence, could be temporary for some Aries. For others this move could be for a much longer duration.

The concept that knowledge is power is extremely relevant for the ambitious Rams. Effort applied to expand your knowledge and skills will pay dividends now and in the future. Even if you are not motivated by professional advancement, you are likely to embrace further study in preparation for a career change or for your own personal satisfaction and self-development. The study of other cultures, law, philosophy, and religion may become of great interest this year. If child care poses a problem for the working Aries mother or father, consider correspondence learning. This can be lifestyle-friendly, and you can access the learning from anywhere in the world.

Jupiter, planet of abundance, is retrograde from early April until early August. Here is an opportunity to review your progress regarding the skills and the knowledge needed to accomplish your goals. Legal and professional people may also play a large part in your life, as your advancement could come through overseas deals and connections. Business profits and the bottom line can be increased through importing and exporting services as well as products. Finance to expand could come from overseas links. However, as an Aries you are prone to impulsiveness. So improved financial stability rests on reducing risks and choosing wise investments.

Saturn, the planet linked to constructive and controlled action, begins the year in the sign of Leo in your sector of self-expression, children, creative endeavors, and romance. Hobbies and leisure pursuits can pay dividends once the hard work is done. The potential to earn extra income through a part-time hobby or artistic pursuit is strengthened. But a tendency to put high expectations on yourself and loved ones will need to be watched. Taking care of children or the elderly may generate a greater load for some Aries. Relationships with older children could begin to change, possibly for the better. Some unemployment, perhaps of your own choosing, as well as financial restrictions could limit your freedom and independence at times because of Saturn's influence.

With Saturn in the romance sector of your solar chart until September, a more serious attitude toward your love life may emerge. Many Aries individuals will search for someone to unite with. Setting up house and settling into a committed union are under good vibes. A potentially fertile period could herald the birth of a child for Aries keen to start a family. For those of you in failing relationships, efforts to rescue and renew love could breathe new life into intimate partnerships. Alternately, decisions may be made to cut the tie and move on. Disclosing to your partner what you desire from your relationship will help to strengthen affection and reinforce emotional bonds. Solo Aries could find new love through friendship, study, and travel or work overseas. Developing a meaningful relationship will soon lead to wedding bells.

This year Mars, your planetary ruler, spends the most amount of time in Cancer, the sign signifying a special relationship to home and family. Mars enters Cancer toward the end of September and remains there until the end of December. Mars in Cancer brings opportunities for home-loving Rams to renovate and refurbish living quarters. It is also an excellent period for Aries looking to move, sell, or buy a home or apartment. And while

Mars is retrograde in Cancer, from mid-November to the end of December, you will have a chance to revisit and revise any plans you have made regarding the home and possible domestic changes.

A healthy mind in a healthy body is the key to well-being. Frequent light meals with plenty of fresh vegetables, fruit, and herbs suit Aries metabolism. In September, when Saturn moves into Virgo and your sixth house of work, health, and service, expect an increased responsibility in these areas. You will then be more inclined to take notice of health and fitness. If you have wanted to improve your stamina and revitalize your health, this is the year that structures can be put in place. Quitting bad habits, introducing a new diet, adopting an exercise program should be much easier. But you must make the effort to change. There could be periods when your workload doubles because of the illness or absence of others. Energy should remain high for much of the forecast period, although this will depend on your willingness to let people help you when you need it.

Anger, anxiety, and negative thinking can slow or block progress. Relaxation techniques as well as natural remedies can be beneficial in quelling the onset of headaches that many Aries are prone to. Taking a sensible approach to all issues of health will lessen the chance of mental and physical stress causing illness. Creative projects, practical hobbies, and leisure pursuits can bring pleasure and also reduce fatigue and tension. Mid-January, May, and September are periods for extra vigilance regarding personal safety. Be careful when traveling and using firearms, sharp tools, and hot appliances.

Uranus, planet of awareness, continues its erratic journey through Pisces in your twelfth house of secret knowledge. Uranus in Pisces contributes to your intellectual growth and also brings the unexpected. Sudden events could alter the way you think. This year many of you are heading for a leap of faith because of changing situations and unexpected developments.

Deceptive Neptune remains in Aquarius in your eleventh house of friends and associates. A little tact could go a long way, enabling you to navigate through potentially tricky situations. Friends or associates could be fickle or deceitful at times, requiring you to remain watchful but not obsessive. There could be changes or an ending with friends or associates. You might decide to drop friends who no longer share your principles. Or there may be a falling-out with some in your circle. Conversely, fresh ideas and pursuits could emerge through contact with interesting new people. Take care that you do not waste money in risky speculation or futile dreams. Not everyone in your friendship circle can be trusted, especially where finances are concerned. So be sensible and don't lend or donate large amounts of money.

When Mercury is retrograde, try to be more concise and aware about all forms of communications. If possible, avoid major decision making. Purchasing large articles is not recommended. Double-check before signing crucial documents, leases, and agreements. Confirm plans and arrangements, as there is more chance of delays and cancellations when Mercury is retrograde. These retrograde periods are February 14 to March 8, June 15 to July 10, and October 12 to November 1.

Pluto, the transformer, has been moving through Sagittarius and your solar ninth house of overseas travel, study, and the higher mind. Higher learning, overseas travel, and people from other countries have a beneficial influence bringing changes of circumstances that you may not expect. Advancement comes by studying the big picture, then making decisions about where your life is headed and whether current aspirations and goals are still relevant. Your twelve months ahead should be filled with action and hope. Use your renowned Aries energy and vitality to best advantage. Begin a new direction with enthusiasm, solve all problems with zeal.

ARIES
DAILY FORECAST: 2007

1st Week/January 1–7

Monday January 1st. Thoughtful communication is the key to your success. This could be a day of short fuses and frayed tempers, so breathe deeply before you blurt out the first thing that comes into your head. Vague directions and unspecified times will plague social gatherings, leaving you driving around unknown areas or waiting for someone. Romance can stimulate you intellectually and change your whole perspective on life.

Tuesday the 2nd. Make sure you haven't forgotten a promise you made. A neighbor could be waiting for your response and won't like being ignored. Finish any tasks such as renovations and gain a feeling of accomplishment. A family feud may be brewing if you are not paying attention. Stop what you are doing now and then to listen to what others are saying, and you will gain a better insight into family dynamics.

Wednesday the 3rd. Today's Full Moon in Cancer puts your personal security in the spotlight. Your boss could be leaning on you too hard and taking up more and more of your time. But if you don't make time for a happy family or home life, you cannot be productive. Speak up for yourself. Your employer needs you as much as you need him or her. Take your loved ones out for some fun and entertainment and enjoy a time to remember.

Thursday the 4th. A spunky colleague can capture your attention and make you wonder. Unable to think clearly or speak coherently, you might be better off declaring your feelings and asking for a date. Budding artists can gain attention and recognition for their work. A new creative project should be left on the drawing board. Forget about it, go out and enjoy yourself, and let the process happen spontaneously.

Friday the 5th. Take the time to thank those who are important to you and who have helped you along the way. The good vibes created will affect you as much as them. You may have to travel to see a friend in need. Don't hesitate, the break will do you good. Take some work with you to fill in what might be empty moments and enjoy the change of scenery. You could win a trip to some exotic and romantic destination.

Saturday the 6th. Don't rush if you can help it, as there will be a lot of holdups along the way to test your patience and perseverance. Aries doesn't usually like to do something twice, but today you might have to redo jobs that you have rushed. A love affair with an older person can blossom, giving you a strength you never knew you had. Children are going to need your guidance, so don't put off what is needed now.

Sunday the 7th. Your expectations can be overexaggerated and stretch your energy reserves to the limit. Take stock, do only what is humanly possible, and leave the rest in the realm of the gods. You never know what might still happen, but you won't bust your boiler over it. Burnout is a common problem for people who care too much. Get a few early nights, break the tedium of your normal routine, and get outdoors for some natural therapy.

Weekly Summary

Put your thoughts down on paper rather than hurt the ones you love. A knack for the poetic may come to the fore and allow you to express the sensitivity and emotion that are deeply felt by Aries. Writers can find a publisher who is interested in publishing your work. But don't let your excitement blind you to the conditions within the contract. You should make sure you, not the publisher, own your work.

A female friend can let you down, so try to be as self-sufficient as possible. The Full Moon will shine a light on any disharmony between your home and career. An alternative to your present lifestyle may show itself and be the answer to your prayers. Don't write off any suggestions as wild ideas until you have looked seriously at all the angles. It might be that something totally unexpected comes into play and changes your life for the better.

This element of the unexpected is likely to turn up in your love life as well. Social gatherings will set the scene for you to be creative and get your ideas out there. Not only will you find you can mix with the best of them, but someone who takes your breath away could start to notice you. Don't let him or her overpower you. Stay in touch with your own needs and sense of self if you want the relationship to be full and lasting.

2nd Week/January 8–14

Monday the 8th. Outside influences and interruptions can put you off your game. Take time to write your schedule for today and stick to it if you want to get anything done. The more businesslike you are the more success you will have. An offer of a leadership role shouldn't be missed. No matter how low your self-confidence is, have a go. Your employer is sure to be watching and will be impressed with your responsible attitude.

Tuesday the 9th. A legal matter can be turned in your favor with the right representation. Don't be afraid to drop your present lawyer if you are not happy with his or her work. Your lover might surprise you with a show of affection, or you may have to help him or her with a difficult social situation. You could decide to tie the knot and dedicate yourself to a lifetime commitment.

Wednesday the 10th. Travel plans can fall into place when a ticket comes your way at half price. Grab what luck gives you today and let everything else take care of itself. A glamorous event this evening can put you in the public eye, so dress to kill and don't let your nerves put you off. Your optimism should be infectious and your dreams within reach. Eradicate all doubts and let your intuition be your guide.

Thursday the 11th. An emotional issue can color your logic and make rational thought difficult. You may read more into a situation than is necessary. Try not to jump to conclusions, especially at work among your colleagues. Confiding in an older and wiser friend can help with any relationship difficulties, as his or her insight can give you a whole new outlook on the matter. Children may need your guidance now.

Friday the 12th. Taking on a large mortgage can stretch your budget and put a strain on a relationship. Talk to your partner about insurance, which will cover you in case of loss of income or illness or death. This safety net can make all the difference. A loved one may be traveling through a country in turmoil, causing you great worry. If you don't hear from the person, contact your embassy for help.

Saturday the 13th. Peer pressure will be subtle and hard to avoid. Choose your company wisely today to eliminate the risk of ending up in a compromising or awkward situation. A romance may have had its day. Weigh the advantages against the costs. You might be stifling your own creative energies for the sake of love. Ask yourself if this relationship is worth it. You may be sacrificing your own well-being.

Sunday the 14th. An emotional confrontation can clear the air early and leave you footloose and fancy-free for the rest of the day. An art or cultural exhibition will be a lot of fun for you and the whole family. Go along and laugh and cry at the myriad possibilities of life's expressions on display. A well-known spiritual teacher could be speaking nearby. Attend the talk and be open to broadening your horizons.

Weekly Summary

Put some thought into your lifestyle. You will intuitively know what you should change to enhance your health and vitality as well as your enjoyment of life. Look at such philosophies as macrobiotics, in which balance is the driving force. It may help you to understand areas where you are overdoing and others where you are lacking. A more holistic lifestyle may be the result.

An old relationship can haunt you and leave its mark on your present one. Reflect on your emotional issues and be open to counseling if life seems less enjoyable than before. It is amazing how more understanding will turn your life around. Your competitive nature can make compromise hard, especially if those in your life are not complying with your expectations.

Friends and acquaintances could be taking up a lot of your time. This may suit you, but be careful that you aren't running after others because you want to be part of the group. Your need to merge with others and bond with your peers could be stronger than your own ambitions. Take a long look at where you are going and adjust your course. Then you will be on the road to success.

3rd Week/January 15–21

Monday the 15th. Social connections are likely expanding, putting you in touch with people from all walks of life and experiences. Be open to the differences and you will benefit. Be judgmental and you might have to wear your own judgments. A chance at a teaching position could mean moving away. Talk it over with your family, and you might be surprised to find they are right behind you and also excited about it.

Tuesday the 16th. Don't allow self-destructive emotions to bring you down and influence your decisions. Remember, it is always darkest before the dawn, and a change may be just about to occur. A self-awareness course could be right up your alley. You will enjoy the challenge of working in a group situation. All types of obstacles will arise in moving toward your dreams, but you can overcome them all.

Wednesday the 17th. Your ruler Mars, the planet of energy and action, has moved into Capricorn in your career sector, imbuing you with the competitive edge to go after your goals. Take the initiative now, start making the changes you want, and set the wheels of success in motion. An altercation with a colleague can make your emotions public. If you don't want others to know your personal business, avoid confrontations and emotional situations.

Thursday the 18th. Your easygoing attitude can make you fair game for more ruthless people. Don't let them ruffle your feathers. A new cycle is beginning, and if you concentrate on what is important to you, you can achieve your own ends, not somebody else's. Accept all the professional challenges that come your way, and you won't have cause for regrets. Instead, you might have cause for celebration.

Friday the 19th. Humanitarian issues can override your personal needs now. You could be willing to give up your free time to work for a good cause. Consider putting pen to paper and spreading your message through newspapers. Or contact local radio stations for an on-air interview. Even if you are pushing your own environmentally friendly business, the more people who hear about it the better it will be for the environment and your business.

Saturday the 20th. A female friend can give you the support you need to get through a difficult situation. Don't be afraid to unload your inhibitions. It will free you up to move on, and your confidence will be safe with her. A busy social schedule could be blocking your creative energy, taking you away from the things that matter. Don't let the need for friendship get in the way of your personal ideals, as this is a time to focus on your dreams.

Sunday the 21st. The value of your friendships and other group efforts can start to become important. Evaluate what is important or relevant to you and your own ideals. Avoid sacrificing values and ideals simply to fit in with others. A friend who is going through a relationship breakup may need more of your time. Get away for the day if you can and take your lover for a long drive through romantic and inspiring scenery.

Weekly Summary

The deeper meaning of life will take on more significance. A friend could introduce you to a spiritual philosophy that inspires and transforms how you look at the world. A spiritual teacher may appear and lecture on aspects of life's journey, which will answer some important questions for you. Or you could travel through a country that opens your eyes to a totally different way of being. Whatever it is, you won't look at the world in quite the same way again.

A career move could be on the cards. Your competitive urge will come into play, and any chance to pit your skill and ingenuity against others will be welcomed. Midweek is an excellent time to start something new, especially a business of your own.

Saturday the Sun moves into Aquarius in your social sector, joining Mercury, Venus, Neptune, and Chiron already there. You can expect the next month to dish up lots of group situations, new friendships, and the chance to make some important contacts for the future. Single Aries may meet a new love and be introduced to a new social set. Other Aries might start to take a leading role in an organization that has an innovative effect on your life.

4th Week/January 22–28

Monday the 22nd. Someone may be trying to undermine your good work. Keep your ideas to yourself, and work behind the scenes to get what you want and to be on the safe side. A female friend could be a thorn in your side. Avoid having anything to do with her right now. The excitement of many social engagements can wear off and become boring. Send your respects and take the evening off for your own enjoyment.

Tuesday the 23rd. Let off steam in a neutral environment to avoid dealing with misunderstandings. A strenuous workout at the gym or a jog in the park might be the most beneficial activities for your mood. This is a day for initiating new ideas and projects. Try changing some of your habits that have outlived their usefulness. Give your personal appearance a lift by getting into the latest fashions and adding more color to your wardrobe.

Wednesday the 24th. Optimism and good cheer can make the most tedious of chores easy. Your wit and fast talk can have your colleagues in stitches. Relations between siblings are likely to be more open and honest than previously. Speculation can be successful if you make wise choices and don't listen to shifty characters. A new romance can make you feel like a new person and add to your self-confidence and success.

Thursday the 25th. A chance encounter at work could give you the opening to make a good impression. Don't let the moment pass by. Compulsive buying can blow your budget. Buying on interest-free terms with no re-payments for a lengthy period just puts the agony off until later. An elderly parent may need you to take control of his or her welfare. Check out all the available options for elder care before you decide what to do.

Friday the 26th. Be sure you have the facts before you make public statements on anything. The risk of missing the point or getting your facts mixed up is strong. Your sensitivity to the moods of others is high, so be smart and avoid negative or depressed people. A friend may need your help, but don't let him or her impose unnecessarily on your kind heart. Self-indulgence can lead to false impressions.

Saturday the 27th. A powerful or influential contact will be a great help to you if you bother to ask. Visit the local markets and enjoy the community atmosphere. Besides picking up unique wares, you might run into someone very important. A neighbor may impose on you to drive him or her to a function. If you go along, you could end up having the time of your life meeting new people and experiencing something different.

Sunday the 28th. The prospect of air travel can set your nerves on edge. You may have to head overseas to visit an ailing friend or loved one. Try aromatherapy to allay your jitters and put you in a relaxed frame of mind. The possibility of studying through long-distance education could be the solution to attaining your goals. Or you might decide to leave your small town and head for the big city to reach for your dreams.

Weekly Summary

The need for privacy and a certain amount of seclusion will give way to your normal gregarious and impulsive mood as the Moon moves into your own sign of Aries. Concentrating on your appearance can spark an expensive spending spree but result in gorgeous new additions to your wardrobe. If you are aware of the subconscious moods that are driving your actions, you will have more control over the outcome.

Your personal feelings of self-worth can get a lift with the offer of a dynamic position working in an area of your choice. You may come into the public eye over an issue you are passionate about. If you have to make a speech, research meticulously to ensure you will be taken seriously. Otherwise your impulsive side could lead you into a situation that is out of your control and inevitably lead to your reputation suffering.

Social events may put you out of your comfort zone but will enhance your prospects for the future. Take care when driving and avoid drinking too much. Your judgment could be impaired and ruin your enhanced status. A secret romance could blossom behind closed doors. Be honest with yourself about the situation and your expectations to avoid feeling let down and hurt.

5th Week/January 29–February 4

Monday the 29th. Look on the bright side and intense emotions won't get the better of you. Aries travelers may find themselves in a situation without an interpreter. Make sure all your papers are in order before crossing borders. An attack of homesickness can result in long letters, phone calls, or e-mails to the family back home. An introduction to your in-laws could be overwhelming, so be prepared for the unexpected and the unusual.

Tuesday the 30th. Throw yourself into the housework early. Once you have imposed order on your environment, your mood will pick up enormously. For a favorable outcome, do your homework on projects or initiatives before acting. Interest in political or environmental change can motivate you to work behind the scenes gathering information and support. Don't be flattered or cajoled into taking a leadership position just yet.

Wednesday the 31st. Take it easy today, as your energy levels could be low, and without rest and good nutrition you are in danger of falling victim to depression. Singles might want to visit their folks. The extra support gained from parents will help you to stay focused on your dreams. Aries sharing a place might feel inspired to cook a feast that helps to create a home atmosphere as well as a sense of family.

Thursday February 1st. Get out your party gear and get set for fun, as today should be a real humdinger. Even if you feel unusually shy and reserved when all eyes turn in your direction, it won't take you long to warm to the moment. Creative activities will star, so get out your paintbrushes, tools, or whatever else you are into and enjoy yourself. Of course, you might fall in love instead.

Friday the 2nd. Nothing is impossible if you put your mind to it. Believe in your ability to create your own reality. Whatever you do, don't play the helpless victim, or else that is what you will become. Own your own power and shape your own destiny. Big changes are in the air, so let go of your fears and start flying like an eagle. Book a trip or enroll in a course for the sheer fun of it.

Saturday the 3rd. Open-air activities will do you a world of good. Go for a run, ask a friend to share a sport, or join the crowd at an exciting spectacle. You may be a little under the weather, so take some vitamins and curl up with a good book after your walk. An old flame could call and remind you of past memories and regrets.

Sunday the 4th. An impending exam or trial of some sort can have you on tenterhooks and unable to keep your mind on anything. Practice deep breathing and wear some lavender oil for relaxation and rosemary oil for your memory, and you will be fine. Success is assured, so don't sabotage yourself. A pet could go missing, so make your companion safe before you go out for the day.

Weekly Summary

Watch your step, as you could be prone to impulsive behavior that even you find a tad excessive. Anybody that pushes your buttons is bound to receive a good serve in return. A busy schedule and not enough time to do things will contribute to your stress load. Keep within the speed limit out on the roads and keep notes on all your business transactions, as you are likely to be moving too fast to absorb all the information.

February opens on a Full Moon in Leo, which will highlight fun and laughter and could herald a new love affair or the start of a creative project. Aries couples who want to start a family may have some luck also. Your confidence and enthusiasm should be high, and you could end up putting yourself center stage at a social event. Be responsible for your actions and you will have nothing to worry about.

Over the weekend relax and unwind from stress. Take a stroll around town and treat yourself to a nourishing meal at a gourmet health-food café or hike along a scenic route for the healing exhilaration for which the great outdoors is famous. Take someone you love and share a heart-to-heart along the way.

6th Week/February 5–11

Monday the 5th. Your daily grind could really bring you down. It may seem as if you are stuck in a depressing dead-end job that offers no opportunity for advancement. This mood will pass, but for now call a friend rather than wallow in pity. Opportunity can arrive through a friend who needs your help. Be ready to help no matter how tedious the problem may sound.

Tuesday the 6th. Take matters into your own hands and avoid being caught up in another's indecision. This is an excellent time to patch up an argument with a friend and heal past hurts. Your partner may seem withdrawn and not his or her usual self. Lend quiet support, but whatever you do, don't take it personally. It will just add to your partner's feelings of insecurity and a seeming lack of support from you.

Wednesday the 7th. High ideals and a sense of empowerment are likely to influence your moves. Meetings will be full of high energy and the inclination to cooperate. Take this opportunity to finalize agreements and contracts. But be sure to read all the fine print, as there is bound to be something you didn't know about. A private fantasy with a colleague could take your mind off important issues.

Thursday the 8th. Flashes of insight can give you a psychological edge, so trust your gut feelings. You may become privy to a secret that will be an ace up your sleeve. Romance is in the air, and unsolicited attention can leave you gasping for breath. You may even find yourself caught up in a triangle of deception. First ask yourself if this is what you want.

Friday the 9th. Adolescent children often buck the system and some Aries parents may be the recipients of a letter from the principal. Rather than lose your cool, remember your own youth and guide the young ones with empathy and understanding. Membership fees could be on the rise, forcing you to consider whether your group is worth it. Still, you've got to have some fun and relaxation.

Saturday the 10th. Think twice about pursuing a lawsuit. It could backfire and result in lots of costs. If you want a psychic reading, check out the medium thoroughly beforehand or postpone the reading until another day. Debts may be weighing on your mind. Don't put them in the too-hard basket, work out a repayment plan with enough left for you to relax and have some fun.

Sunday the 11th. If you are trying to make an impression on those whom you admire, you are better off relaxing and just enjoying their company. Any attempt at pretense can have the opposite effect. A friend may be twisting the truth and turning you against another. Look at actions, not words, for a reality check on the situation. High expectations can change into disappointment this evening.

Weekly Summary

Since work matters could come to a head, refuse to be intimidated or coerced into taking sides. Instead, stick to the cold, hard facts and say what you think. Only through openness and honesty can troublemakers be exposed and the problems resolved once and for all. Your partner might be giving you a hard time over a child's behavior. If you can't resolve the disagreements, seek mediation.

This can be a frustrating time, and you could buckle under the competitive pressure that goes with your chosen career. A superior who likes you as a friend is on your side and can give you a few tips on winning. Listen to everything said, and you will know intuitively what to do. It might be time for you to learn how good you really are and start to have confidence in your own abilities.

Your usual social circle can start to lack luster and become basically unsatisfying. Go out by yourself and explore other avenues for entertainment. A personal creative interest might give you a break from the merry-go-round of Saturday nights and also leave your bank balance intact. This will impress your bank manager in your favor when you next ask for a loan.

7th Week/February 12–18

Monday the 12th. A vacation may be long overdue. Why not arrange a trip and get away for a while? Give yourself a break and stop trying to please everybody all the time. Start a course in metaphysics and escape the mundane or try some writing to enhance your lifestyle. The world is your oyster. Don't let self-doubt and recriminations hold you back from realizing your dreams.

Tuesday the 13th. Bite the bullet and trust your inner strength today. Aries can be changeable. But that doesn't mean you don't have the commitment to see things through and gain a sense of achievement. Just be patient while Mercury goes retrograde tonight until March 8. An important business decision should be made alone. Advice from outsiders will only confuse matters. Make your partner feel like royalty by giving an early valentine treat.

Wednesday the 14th. You will get a lot done today if you focus on your objectives. Don't let interruptions distract you, or you could end up somewhere else doing something totally different. You can expect to be on the road a bit, so put some relaxing music in the car to keep your cool. A creative talent might turn into a real moneymaker. Don't shy away from any propositions that come your way.

Thursday the 15th. Watch out for friends who know no limits. Their wild and freedom-loving spirits may be exciting, but you could end up with a whole lot of trouble. A sudden urge for change will lead you to greener pastures. Accept an invitation from a colleague, even if you think you are out of your depth. Stepping out with someone different will be better than a breath of fresh air.

Friday the 16th. Aries are always on the go and can suffer from burnout more often than others. Visit a natural therapist and make sure you get the vitamins and minerals that are right for your system. Consider your codependency on friends and groups and assess whether you are really and truly fulfilled or not. If not, a spiritual group may be more beneficial now.

Saturday the 17th. The New Moon in Aquarius lights up your social sector and can spark a new interest in humanitarian or environmental ideals. Get involved in your local area and see the difference firsthand. As the saying goes, think global, act local. A relationship may have recently broken up, leaving you footloose and fancy-free. Don't rush into anything too soon. Enjoy your newfound independence.

Sunday the 18th. Nervous energy can affect your moods, making them go up and down like a yo-yo. Jump in a hot tub and soak an hour away. Listen to your favorite music or burn some relaxing oils and practice your breathing. Visitors in the afternoon can disturb your peace and quiet but also add stimulation and camaraderie. Go with the flow.

Weekly Summary

High ideals and aspirations can turn into disappointments if you try to take on too much. Keep your ambitions in tune with reality and be happy to achieve a bit at a time. You can make the changes you need eventually. Your energy will be focused on achieving your goals, and this could put you in the hot seat at work. Make sure you don't step on the toes of colleagues as you scramble to prove that you are the best.

Aries students may be getting to know the people of their sorority or fraternity, experiencing the fear and elation of a new group identity. A person from the past can turn up on your doorstep with tall tales and true of their traveling adventures. You may have the chance to choose the company you mix with now, and this choice will affect your future. Put yourself first and don't be led around by the nose.

At the weekend you will be looking for a retreat. Think about getting away for a couple of days and relaxing. If you have friends who live out in the sticks, give them a call. You can catch up with them and have a break without expending too much energy and money. This might be a good time to start planning an overseas adventure by reading about faraway places you might visit.

8th Week/February 19–25

Monday the 19th. A close bond with a female friend could hit a few bumps today. A difference of opinion can sabotage your friendship if you let it. Practice forgiveness if you can. A change of heart can affect an important decision. Make sure you are not letting another's wishes or fears about the outcome sway your resolve. Later your mood will lift, and the evening will be a time of fun.

Tuesday the 20th. Today could be the start of something big. A creative venture can get under way now, and success looks to be assured. You are likely to be setting off on a long journey that will change your life forever. Your partner's family may live overseas, and you are going to meet them for the first time. A move farther away can open up new avenues of creativity you have never dreamed of.

Wednesday the 21st. Venus, planet of love and harmony, now moves into your own sign of Aries and will stay there for the next three weeks. This should put you at your best, bringing romance into your life or a new artistic project that adds to your own attractiveness. You will want to add value to your surroundings as well, and could overstretch your budget on new possessions. Try to maintain a balance.

Thursday the 22nd. Step outside your hectic schedule, if only for an hour, and reflect on the things that truly inspire you. If you always follow where your heart leads, you can't go wrong. Material possessions may start to lose their luster when compared to your freedom, creativity, and need for love. Nevertheless, you still need to keep your feet firmly on the ground if you are going to achieve any of these things.

Friday the 23rd. Things should be coming together well enough for you to give yourself a pat on the back. Contracts and agreements can seem to be held up interminably. But after March 7, when Mercury moves forward again, they should proceed without any problems. Finding time to attend a night class that will improve your prospects may be hard, but you can find a way. Just don't worry about it.

Saturday the 24th. A cross-cultural relationship can make you feel isolated and alone. Visit a close friend and get things off your chest. Relationships are meant to be a two-way street of giving and taking, not one person giving and the other taking. Leave your car at home and walk through the neighborhood, chatting with the locals.

Sunday the 25th. A brother or sister may need your support. If you haven't heard from him or her for a while, it might be wise to call. Student teachers could receive a training post that will test your skills to the limit. Racial issues, violence, and drugs might all be high profile. Aries writers can receive negative feedback from publishers. You may need to try a publisher who deals in your specific genre.

Weekly Summary

Concentrate on yourself! Add a dash of flair with a stylish hat or head scarf. You might even update your eyeglass frames if you wear glasses. Wear colors such as soft reds and golds to bring out your vivacious and warm nature. Others will be much more responsive to you, so take the opportunity to ask for help and the things you need. You won't be turned down.

A relationship may not be giving you what you want. Before you start an argument, try a cooperative approach and be honest about your expectations of your partner. Take the time to notice what his or her needs are and give your partner more time. Buy a gift to make your lover feel special and open up the channel of communication. Love is like a flower. If you don't water it, the bloom withers.

Students should make sure they keep up with the work, or you will be in danger of falling behind and missing something important. A study group would be an advantage. You can discuss your topic and look at it from all sides as the other students express their understanding. Keep up to date with your paperwork too. An important letter or message could be mislaid and put you at a disadvantage.

9th Week/February 26–March 4

Monday the 26th. Take things easy today and give yourself space to think. Family matters may have reached a head, but nobody wants to put his or her feelings into words. A home beautification project could have stalled, leaving you frustrated with the mess. Rearrange the furniture to make comfort a priority, and please the whole family with a favorite take-out for dinner.

Tuesday the 27th. Thoughts from the past can replay over and over in your head. People you are trying to contact may not be there. Don't drown your sorrows or wallow in self-pity. Sit down and write out your thoughts. You might be surprised where they lead you. Volunteer for a charity group and gain comfort from helping those far worse off than you.

Wednesday the 28th. This should be a high-energy day with plenty of activities to keep you busy. Your ability to find solutions to problems will be in fine form, and friends might call on you to help them out in various ways. You should be selective though, as there are only so many hours in the day. The temptation to speed should be avoided, and so should your tendency to play rescuer. Romance is on the cards this evening.

Thursday March 1st. Saturn, planet of hard luck, is currently opposing Neptune, the confusing chameleon of the zodiac. This can convey anxiety and disorientation. It is also a perfect atmosphere for people to take advantage, so beware! Your money is much safer in the bank than invested in risky speculative ventures that promise a lot but deliver little. Losses are also likely if you are trying to beat the odds at the gaming tables.

Friday the 2nd. A small social gathering could develop into an outrageous party. Don't fret if your housework is not up to par. If your guests are friends, they are unlikely to take any notice, and you have the whole weekend to restore order. Take a fresh and sensible look at your eating habits. Discard those that no longer fit into your new lifestyle or which could endanger your well-being.

Saturday the 3rd. Negative aspects prevail in the cosmos that could contribute to poor health and to issues with coworkers. The eclipsed Full Moon in Virgo may affect your general well-being, possibly bringing minor issues you need to take care of. If you don't have to be at work, find a relaxing pastime that is both enjoyable and doesn't require a lot of thought or energy.

Sunday the 4th. You may have to face the temptation to overindulge. Pace yourself with everything you do, and a pleasant day is in store. A chatty mood prevails, but make sure that what you say is relevant as well as interesting. Restrict socializing to locations close to home. Otherwise you may become tired and cranky contending with travel delays or other problems with transportation.

Weekly Summary

The week begins with your ruler Mars heading into quirky Aquarius and your zone of friendships and future goals. Although this should assist drive and motivation to bring aims to fruition, be aware of the motives of others. Now is not the time to rashly invest in ventures that you haven't thoroughly investigated or to gamble with your resources.

If you are feeling off for a few days, it may be your body telling you to slow down. It is unlikely to be anything serious, but if you have persistent ailments, it would be advisable to seek appropriate treatment. Take advantage of rest breaks when working. You will need breaks to keep motivation up. It might be time to schedule a visit to the dentist, especially if you have been putting it off.

Saturday an eclipsed Full Moon in Virgo advises care with the emotions and feelings of others, especially people who are more sensitive than you, such as your Cancer, Scorpio, or Pisces friends. Expect to encounter travel problems and delays. Factor this possibility in when making arrangements to meet people right after work.

10th Week/March 5–11

Monday the 5th. A slip of the tongue by a coworker could be very revealing. Listen carefully, but play along as if you didn't hear or suspect a thing. This information could be invaluable at a later time. Unexpected events are likely to throw a monkey wrench in the works. Make sure your agenda is flexible so you can easily cope with any contingencies that are likely to come your way.

Tuesday the 6th. A talent for spotting a bargain could provide extra income for you. Defer plans to purchase a plane ticket for an upcoming vacation until later in the week. If you purchase now you will probably pay too much. Difficulties within an intimate relationship could arise throughout most of the day. However, relations should improve by tonight. Defer partnership discussions until later on.

Wednesday the 7th. Many obstacles you have confronted over the past three weeks should be easier to overcome once Mercury goes direct at midnight tonight. Personal goals you have shelved might be worth another look just to make sure that they are no longer as important to you as they once were. Socializing with loved ones or friends could be high on the agenda tonight.

Thursday the 8th. Take advantage of opportunities to develop your talents and skills, in particular your ability to speak in public. Get up and talk if asked. Increasing confidence in speaking expands your capacity in many job-related areas, and boosts self-confidence. Potential romance could be found at a business function that also includes a social activity. Couples should share a happy rapport.

Friday the 9th. This is a day when you will be more interested in seeking pleasure rather than engaging in serious activities. Aries with artistic abilities could be inspired to create a masterpiece that brings your skills to the notice of others. Singles could fall in love quickly, which may not be the best decision you have ever made. It would be better to let things develop at a much slower and casual pace.

Saturday the 10th. Reviewing bank statements or organizing tax documents may be boring, but it is a positive way to utilize today's planetary trends. If you discover any complicated problems, consulting a bank official or financial adviser should prove beneficial. The anticipation of a long-planned vacation is building. Take care of any last-minute arrangements early so you are not confronted with problems closer to your departure.

Sunday the 11th. Disruptive influences could be at work this morning. Go with the flow and avoid becoming embroiled in arguments with relatives or your lover. Aries likes to be on the move, so if you feel you are in a rut, don't lounge around at home. Go window-shopping, visit your folks, or meet friends for a late breakfast. A trip to a theme park or the zoo could be an outing for parents and children to enjoy.

Weekly Summary

Unpredictable influences prevail with the Sun and Uranus conjunct in Pisces in your sector of personal limitations and charitable undertakings. Situations of a secretive nature may need to be dealt with swiftly, or a confidential issue could come to light, taking everyone by surprise. Take notice of your dreams, as innovative solutions to outstanding problems could be revealed in a unique manner.

A family member or someone close could contribute a large amount of money to assist your current plans or goals. Be careful when handling equipment or machinery that may not be working efficiently. Breakdowns are likely to occur and will test both your patience and resolve. Spend some time satisfying your need to be among beautiful artwork, sculptures, or paintings.

Pay attention to plans concerning an upcoming vacation. A family member or a friend who is accompanying you may need to be contacted to confirm last-minute arrangements. With the ability to sell yourself, mixing business with pleasure could produce an interesting challenge that should pay handsome dividends.

11th Week/March 12–18

Monday the 12th. Make contact with any relatives or friends you suspect are lonely or you know will be spending the day alone. Assisting those who may be gloomy and down in the dumps can be a great way to receive emotional satisfaction. Higher education or issues concerning publishing could occupy some of your time. Attending conferences and workshops is likely to provide a valuable source of business information.

Tuesday the 13th. You may need to make a decision concerning your business or employment affairs. Consider all your options thoroughly before coming to definite conclusions, especially if your decision impacts on others. If family affairs need to be considered, ask advice of those who will be objective. Self-image should be strong because of the consideration and kind words of someone you respect.

Wednesday the 14th. Seek out different forms of entertainment or a change of routine to overcome any gloomy feelings. Produce a business plan if you need to raise funds for expansion or to develop a new commercial enterprise. Receiving support from others will be easier once they see your professional approach. Working your way up the ladder is likely to come quicker if you are employed in a large corporation.

Thursday the 15th. Be selective with your choice of friends now. Not all newcomers to your circle will be enamored by your charm or you by theirs. Throughout the next few days, stop long enough to pursue your ideas, thoughts, and imagination. You may find that a new invention or different way of performing a task could form, leading to increased productivity and income.

Friday the 16th. Your magnetic charm can be displayed to your advantage. Wear your best business outfit if you are out to claim the attention of someone influential. Once you are noticed, then you can impress with your skills and abilities. Pay attention when interacting with others. An opportunity too good not to follow up may be presented. If you are not listening, something could slip by unnoticed.

Saturday the 17th. A charitable or kind act is likely to be returned just when your need is the greatest. Give what you can and wait to be rewarded. Lovely Venus now visits her own sign of Taurus, bringing attention to your personal monetary zone. Making plans to increase financial resources and add to your possessions may occupy your time as you consider various ways to put your fertile ideas into action.

Sunday the 18th. With a cluster of planets in Pisces in your zone of secrets, something is about to be revealed, even if this is not what you want or expect. Mercury joining the Sun, Uranus, and the Pisces New Moon is sure to bring hidden issues to the attention of busybodies or others' prying eyes. Create more time for private activities that you enjoy, especially if the majority of your time is spent on assisting other people.

Weekly Summary

Aries should be in a compassionate frame of mind, eager to provide help and service wherever assistance is needed. Friendly overtures given to those who may be feeling a bit low will be appreciated. The added benefit will be raising the spirits of those you help as well as your own. If you have a secret, it may be better to fess up now, as it is likely to come out when you least expect it.

Pace yourself. There is no need to stop planned activities. Just make sure you don't expend all your energy on one task or event. Dress to impress, and success is bound to come your way. Obtaining special clients' accounts or a promotion could be your reward. As an Aries you like change, so try a variety of different forms of entertainment or hobby activities to keep boredom at bay.

End-of-week planetary movement produces a change of atmosphere. Venus enters her home sign of Taurus, positively highlighting your sector of personal finances. Talkative Mercury enters placid Pisces and your solar twelfth sector, providing the impetus for you to quietly complete leftover chores and obligations, which can bring an immense sense of relief.

12th Week/March 19–25

Monday the 19th. Don't discuss business or commercial secrets with anyone until you confirm that everyone is on the same team. Don't take sides if you are called upon to sort out a family problem behind the scenes. Even if you are not in a party mood, invite your best buddies around to share in your casual and relaxed hospitality. You deserve to have some fun now.

Tuesday the 20th. An action-packed month ahead is likely with today's entry of the Sun into your sign of Aries and your personality sector. Energy should be high, providing the motivation for you to power forward with personal projects and plans. Enthusiasm and optimism can propel you to high achievements. The more you focus on your potential, the more momentum you will gather.

Wednesday the 21st. Today is a day for having fun even if you are on the job. Some luck is surrounding you, although you are unlikely to end up with any more money than you have now. It could be a case of easy come and easy go, especially if you are in a gambling mood. But take advantage of cosmic luck and share a lottery ticket with your coworkers. You might even enter a magazine contest.

Thursday the 22nd. Make a concerted effort to spend less and save more. A conservative approach can help you move ahead, especially if you have been overly extravagant lately. A friend or several friends may be deliberately vague or even prone to deceiving you now. It might be better to skip plans to socialize, as you could spend your time seething with resentment at their disloyalty.

Friday the 23rd. A close friend could provide the inspiration to start you researching your family tree or making contact with long-lost relatives. A few inquiries in the right place could assist you in tracking down relevant information. A writing or research project could bring lots of enjoyment, with Aries authors making good progress with literary works.

Saturday the 24th. Numerous e-mails or phone calls are likely to keep you on the go throughout the day. Sharing ideas or brainstorming with those in your circle could prove very productive. Write your to-do list first thing this morning, and you should manage to complete a large number of tasks quickly and efficiently. A love affair may have to withstand an enforced period of separation.

Sunday the 25th. Letting go of issues raised through a family drama may not be easy but is essential for your general feeling of well-being. Resist the spiels of persistent salespeople if you are shopping. Even if an item is a bargain, refuse to be pressured into buying something nonessential or that you don't really need right now. Spending for the sake of it doesn't help you or your bank balance.

Weekly Summary

Self-inflicted pressure and stress could mark the beginning of this week. It will be essential to remain cool and calm with whatever situations confront you. Even though you could be tempted, don't challenge those in authority at least until next week. You are likely to come out on the losing end. Participating in a spiritual pursuit could be extremely helpful in reducing tension.

Take plenty of time to get to know newcomers to your social circle before involving them fully in your activities. A shared rapport could possibly be lacking, which could make conditions slightly uncomfortable. If you are seeking favors from others, you should be successful this week. Make sure your requests are feasible, and your wishes should be readily granted.

Happy Birthday, Aries! The Sun will shine brightly in your sign March 20 to April 20. Make sure you get together with family and friends to celebrate and have fun during the four weeks of your solar return. Aries energy is about moving forward, so don't let any negative comments or situations stop your progression. A group outing may be the scene for a romantic encounter.

13th Week/March 26–April 1

Monday the 26th. Your head could be in the clouds today, ensuring that concentration will most certainly be lacking. If you feel you are in a rut, begin a household project that requires a creative input. Make sure you enlist the assistance of family members so the job is completed before you run out of steam. Ask a special companion to share your hospitality this evening.

Tuesday the 27th. Changes are in store for you now. There is a danger for impulsive Aries in thinking that a new lover is just perfect in every way. It may come as a shock when you realize that this is not a realistic attitude. No one is perfect, so wake up to this fact sooner rather than later. Defer a shopping trip if this was in your plans, as you are unlikely to find any good deals and will wonder why you wasted your time.

Wednesday the 28th. The mail may bring some disturbing news, possibly relating to financial affairs. Perhaps the credit-card statement is a lot larger than you anticipated. Time to call a halt to the spending spree if you want to pay the monthly bills. It might feel as if there are never enough hours in the day to complete your ever growing workload. A night at home and early to bed instead of a social outing might be the answer to lethargy.

Thursday the 29th. Don't provoke others this morning, or you will feel their wrath. Aries will be seeking excitement and stimulating interaction, especially regarding social plans. A sparkling romantic possibility could stir up emotional energies for the unattached. You who are in a permanent union should be prepared for changes that are unexpected but which could bring a new level of understanding to your relationship.

Friday the 30th. Aries venturing out to party this evening needs to be discerning. Keep behavior at social gatherings under control. You don't want to be embarrassed when you hear of your exploits tomorrow. You may be inclined to loosen inhibitions or act in a reckless manner. Desiring a break from your usual routine could make you more than willing to experiment with different activities and pursuits.

Saturday the 31st. Lightning-quick decisions involving your love life are likely today. These may be impulsive and not very well thought out. But good fortune is smiling, so everything should turn out for the best. You could find yourself wondering how come you are so lucky just now. The cosmos is in a jovial mood, so lap it up. A financial boost or surprise could also be on the horizon.

Sunday April 1st. It may not be your best day, as current trends are not conducive to cooperation from associates or friends. Remaining cool, calm, and collected may be extremely difficult for the impulsive Ram. Rise to the challenge, and don't let the taunts of others get under your skin. With your nerves on edge, tomorrow could find you apologizing to those you upset today.

Weekly Summary

Thought processes are likely to be muddled as you begin this week. A lack of concentration limits your ability to focus on detailed or tedious work. Craving excitement and variety could produce problems if you have to fulfill mundane and routine chores. Use your imagination and creative skills to instill fun and magic into your routine to keep boring jobs interesting.

Irritability and anxiety are likely to emerge, bringing a sense of dejection. If this happens, think about your positive achievements. Physical stamina may be below par, cautioning you to take a good look at the condition of your body. Infections might be a problem, so take appropriate action to avoid cuts and burns. Consider participating in new leisure pursuits, which may open up new opportunities.

Happiness and emotional highs are likely for Rams deeply in love. For singles a romantic encounter could brighten your love life. Finding stimulating activities to keep you occupied may prove to be an interesting challenge. As an Aries you have a tendency to begin many projects at once, and you don't always get around to completing them.

14th Week/April 2–8

Monday the 2nd. A tense atmosphere prevails. The Libra Full Moon conveys a warning to be gentle with the feelings of those who hold a significant place in your heart. Look to see where changes can be implemented if a romantic relationship is currently in trouble. Solutions could be found if you tread warily. Personal powers are heightened, so take advantage of opportunities for self-promotion.

Tuesday the 3rd. Optimism and idealism remain high, although accepting that you have creative talent could be a problem. There may be a tendency to continually underestimate capabilities, which in turn stops your progress. Messages are subject to misunderstandings, mix-ups, and confusion. Aries students and writers need to ensure that wording is clear, concise, and articulate.

Wednesday the 4th. The prevailing atmosphere is not clear. Today could be good or it could turn out to be a disaster. Stay positive and everything should be okay. However, confusion is the likely outcome if you absorb all the ideas and plans of everyone with whom you communicate. Pay close attention to business matters to reduce errors or problems that are likely to impact your wallet.

Thursday the 5th. Complaints or queries made to a financial institution can be resolved to your satisfaction today. Be persistent. Don't allow others to fob you off until all your questions have been answered. Expansive Jupiter moves into backward motion, giving you the chance to reflect on your aspirations and whether your level of education is sufficient to meet your current goals.

Friday the 6th. Your ruler Mars enters Pisces and your secretive twelfth zone. This phase brings an unusual amount of uneasy and irrational thoughts and feelings to the fore over the next few weeks. During this time your accomplishments will come through working alone rather than as part of a team. You may be more inclined to tire easily. Remember to pace yourself and not leave everything to the last minute. Keeping late nights to a minimum can aid vitality.

Saturday the 7th. It would be wise to wait until issues are clearer before making plans to further your education. An alternative option could arise that will better meet your current needs. Properly thought-out ideas and organization will assist Aries with financial matters or negotiations. Treat all developments regarding your personal funds with discretion and in strict confidence to obtain the best results.

Sunday the 8th. With Mars and Mercury in Pisces in your twelfth sector of self-analysis, Aries will be in a more reflective and contemplative mood. Spending the day quietly engaged in your own activities could be appealing. If family duty calls, opt for entertainment that is peaceful, relaxing, and interesting enough for all to enjoy and learn something new. Finish the day with a relaxing soak or swim to wash your troubles away.

Weekly Summary

All week take care with what you say and how you say it. As an Aries you are usually prone to exaggeration and jumping in, boots and all, before stopping to think. Humility is also not one of your major strengths. Modesty and the ability to think and say the right thing at the right time will be the key to keeping others on your side.

A Libra Full Moon may bring potential confrontation as well as a battle of wills within your intimate relationship. Although romantic emotions and desires are stimulated, trying to express your feelings to a loved one might prove challenging if you lack sensitivity. On the other hand, don't go overboard in an attempt to please others or to be all things to all people. This will run you ragged.

Your ruler Mars visits Pisces and your twelfth house until May 15. It is an appropriate period to catch up on all outstanding obligations and unfinished projects, especially those of a personal nature. Romantic unions may be tested. Those that do survive should be of long duration. A financial offer, deal, or purchase could become a priority and with careful handling could open a door to something larger.

15th Week/April 9–15

Monday the 9th. You should wake up feeling fresh and ready to tackle anything that comes your way. Optimistic plans for the future can be implemented with confidence and poise. Rumors of a company takeover may be gathering momentum, but if true should ultimately be to your benefit. Consider upgrading job skills to be ready for possible shake-ups and to increase future prospects.

Tuesday the 10th. You can complete a work assignment efficiently and with time to spare if effort is applied right from the beginning. Response to your ideas, designs, or drawings could bring enthusiastic reactions from others, especially if you also lay out the practical application of your plans. Some of your old memories are negative. Don't bring them up if you want to avoid a lovers' tiff and retain harmony on the home front.

Wednesday the 11th. Aries certainly won't experience a lack of social invitations and opportunities now that quick-witted Mercury has entered your sign and your personality sector. If you are currently solo, you could meet your match at a community event or through a neighborhood gathering. Creative talent should increase, so be prepared to impress others with your ideas and well-thought-out plans.

Thursday the 12th. A can-do attitude is great, but one thing at a time should be your motto. An offer to assist a business associate is sure to be valued. However, don't underestimate what is expected. Adding too much to an already heavy workload can increase pressure and lead to unwanted anxiety. Disappointment is likely if you are shopping for an upscale outfit for a special occasion. Don't rush. You will find what you are looking for if you wait.

Friday the 13th. Take on strenuous tasks early, as energy will begin to flag around midmorning. Working behind the scenes could prove advantageous later on today. Preparations to unveil a new venture may run into problems in the beginning but should be resolved fairly quickly. Solitary pursuits are favored this evening. Consciousness can be raised through meditation or deep thinking.

Saturday the 14th. Aries can draw on quick-thinking mental skills to engage in interesting and diverse discussions. If speaking to an audience, stick with the topic and don't go off on a tangent. Be prepared to find another activity tonight, as a friend might unexpectedly cancel social plans. Maybe a night at home would be preferable. Some edgy feelings are likely to lessen your need for company.

Sunday the 15th. It may be a strange day. You could begin by feeling emotional or agitated in the morning and totally over it by lunchtime. Take the opportunity to clear things up. Whether this is clutter around the home or a situation of ongoing concern, removing the debris revitalizes your energy. A romantic evening is ahead, with candles, good cutlery, and fine linen even if your culinary expertise is limited.

Weekly Summary

Luck surrounds Aries now. Changes can be implemented if you stay positive and confident in your beliefs. If energy is used sensibly, much can be accomplished now. Keep an open mind and try at least one new thing a day to develop more self-awareness and to bring into your life the spirit of adventure that you crave. Behavior to be more aware of now could include compulsive thoughts.

The tempo of life picks up when Mercury enters Aries in your first house of action, and Venus enters talkative Gemini in your third house of communication. Social invitations and impromptu gatherings will be on the rise, as well as increased interactions with a special person. A tendency to think and speak quickly will require an effort to slow down speech so others can understand what you have to say.

Avoid exhausting physical resources at week's end. The Moon joins Mars and Uranus in Pisces, your solitary twelfth sector. This signals a time for the body to rest for a few days. Defer heavy tasks until next week when energy rebounds. Projects that require sustained energy over a long period would be better left until your ruler Mars comes to its home sign of Aries on May 15.

16th Week/April 16–22

Monday the 16th. An extra boost of vitality and persuasiveness should prove effective, convincing important people that your ideas and plans have merit. This should also generate extra income for you and for your company. As an Aries you could want something done right away without having to wait. However, patience is the key. Asking others for help if you need it is not a weakness but a strength.

Tuesday the 17th. Creating a more up-to-date image comes easier with today's New Moon culminating in your sign of Aries. Sprucing up your wardrobe can be as simple and as inexpensive as adding colorful scarves, unusual fashion jewelry, or an outstanding manicure. Leadership abilities and increased charisma could lead to an offer to take on a project that displays your many talents and expertise, adding a new dimension to your life.

Wednesday the 18th. You may find it hard to admit that balancing the budget is not one of your strengths. Unless you take a long hard look at your spending habits, staying out of debt could remain something you dream about but never realize. Creative potential is high. Creative talent could generate part-time income through a hobby that adds dollars to your savings.

Thursday the 19th. Intense experiences are possible as Saturn, after a long retrograde, goes direct today. Elimination of old structures and habits can be successfully removed. Do whatever it takes to move ahead. It is an excellent day for students and researchers in all fields. A breakthrough could herald a major transformation, which will have long-lasting effects both for you and the community at large.

Friday the 20th. As the Sun enters Taurus and your personal monetary zone, interests involving financial assets and possessions come into the spotlight. Progress can be made if attention is focused on income, expenditures, and finding ways to increase your savings. If your creative output has suffered limitations, you should find that obstacles are shifting, allowing for increased productivity.

Saturday the 21st. Lost items can be found if you explore places where old family mementos are usually stored. You could also find articles you thought had disappeared for good. Increased concentration encourages tasks that require focus and attention to detail to be successfully undertaken. A contract, financial offer, or purchase relating to foreign interests may begin as a hassle but will ultimately be advantageous.

Sunday the 22nd. A spiritual approach to a complex family issue should bring a quick and satisfactory solution. Rams will be easily entertained today, as you could indulge in fantasy or opt for religious pursuits. Strong imagination is at work, but avoid chores or projects that need total focus. Unlike yesterday, your concentration may be lacking. Singles could find a possible romantic interest close to home.

Weekly Summary

There will be plenty of action to keep you busily occupied all week. Aries has the ability to inspire listeners with a public address or lecture as long as you do not deviate from the topic. There may be a tendency to start speaking about one particular issue and then jump to something entirely different, confusing those within earshot.

A new monthly cycle begins with the Aries New Moon. This is an excellent time to begin personal projects that you hope will endure. And Saturn moving forward will give you an opportunity to turn your life around in a positive and transforming way. Consider what is no longer wanted or working in your life, then take steps to make changes for the better.

Lady Luck smiles on you now. This does not necessarily indicate a lottery win, but life should improve and you will feel more contented. Concentration increases as well as organizational abilities. Difficulties finding creative solutions to any problems will be minor, which will please you as well as those with whom you work. Artists, writers, and musicians should experience a flow of imaginative energies that assist progress.

17th Week/April 23–29

Monday the 23rd. Unsettling conditions prevail today as your ruler Mars challenges love goddess Venus. Feeling confident to express physical needs and desires within a relationship can at times be daunting. Communicate your needs to your partner. Unless your lover is aware of your wishes, he or she cannot help. Solo Aries might feel a strong attraction to someone who catches your eye. But be discerning, as a relationship built on desire alone is unlikely to endure.

Tuesday the 24th. Social life is unlikely to be inspiring today, although by evening things could begin to improve. Adverse trends indicate that mixing business with pleasure is not likely to be fruitful and could be damaging. Even your renowned charm may not elicit enough interest in your commercial dealings. It is a good idea to stay on the straight and narrow path without deviating.

Wednesday the 25th. Most of your thoughts could be centered on romantic interests and social pursuits. If worries around a love affair are causing anxiety, try to take a more relaxed approach. With Jupiter, planet of expansion, linking positively with Saturn's energies of common sense, this is a fruitful period for overcoming obstacles and making the correct decision for your future happiness and security. Schedule a reflexology massage to help you unwind.

Thursday the 26th. Venus, planet of love and money, will be confronting Uranus, planet of chaos and disruption, over the next few days. Matters concerning personal freedom versus possessiveness could erupt. Glamorous socializing will be enjoyable this evening, albeit expensive. If money is a problem, you may need to curb extravagant tendencies. Favorite hobbies and interests could also be high on your agenda.

Friday the 27th. Communicative Mercury joins the Sun in Taurus, spotlighting your personal assets until May 11. Money spent on something you think is a waste of resources could turn out to be just the opposite. Don't be discouraged if you haven't been as diligent with your diet and physical exercise as you should be. A new health regimen started now should bring hoped-for improvements.

Saturday the 28th. As your ruler Mars is merging with Uranus, planet of surprises, in Pisces today, expect sudden events or incidents to occur. Energy is high but may not be controlled, causing impulsive or reckless behavior. If your current objective is to save rather than spend money, defer shopping now. Monitor what you eat and observe your diet. Avoid rich and sweet foods.

Sunday the 29th. If you do something wrong or break the law, pleading your case is unlikely to change the opinion of authorities. Pay up and resolve not to make the same mistake again. Emotional upsets with your mate can make this a difficult day. Although you like to talk, deep and meaningful conversations are not your usual choice of entertainment. It's especially so if your actions are being criticized. Exercise patience or find an alternate way to spend your time.

Weekly Summary

Be watchful and careful if you are slightly agitated and out of sorts. With cranky Mars challenging vixen Venus, you are bound to experience unrest within your intimate relationships. Not being in charge of the situation will bring anxiety. It would be better to accept that in this instance you need to relinquish control and take a backseat for a short time.

Singles would be well advised to remember the motto of act in haste, repent at leisure when it comes to your romantic life. Be discerning when engaging in the getting-to-know-you encounters with potential interests. Relationships that begin now may be hot and saucy, but be prepared for the fervor to fizzle out and disappear as quickly as it began.

Best results come if you take one task at a time, something that may be difficult for enterprising Aries. Trying to do everything at once will only make more work in the end, especially if you cut corners to finish quickly. If you slow down, you have the opportunity to make progress in career, business, and domestic matters, as your ability to use logic and common sense is greatly enhanced.

18th Week/April 30–May 6

Monday the 30th. Today brings a different set of energies to those you experienced over the weekend. Creativity and imagination are strong. To use them to your advantage, apply discipline and structure. It's possible that minor accidents could cause health problems if you are too impulsive or careless. Watch what you are doing and where you are going and you can avoid this possibility.

Tuesday May 1st. The risk of accidents remains high if impulsive or rash behavior is not kept in check. Gains can be made if effort is extended to secure the family budget. Taking care of debts, either paying or collecting them, should be a priority to ensure financial stability. A business venture that carries an element of risk should be avoided. Current trends do not support speculation.

Wednesday the 2nd. Today's Scorpio Full Moon is sure to awaken powerful emotions in Aries people. Your moodiness may be the cause of friction with someone close over issues involving personal or joint finances. Becoming angry with others who don't share your vision about how household income should be spent is an exercise in futility. Instead, work out a household budget that everyone can live with.

Thursday the 3rd. A property contract might fall through today, possibly because of a lack of funds. Delays or errors in paperwork could also hold up involvement in a legal action. Negotiations regarding a business partnership, although seemingly friendly, may not be weighted in your favor now. Defer accepting any deals until you are sure that you are receiving your rightful dues.

Friday the 4th. Romantic Venus clashes with possessive Pluto, bringing hidden passions, jealousy, and desires to the surface. Compulsiveness or extra demands involving your intimate relationship need to be avoided. Otherwise, trouble could erupt, even in committed unions. Singles should choose lovers wisely. Career and money matters make progress through a positive and practical attitude regarding personal responsibilities.

Saturday the 5th. This will not be a boring day for Aries. Good fortune and unexpected situations are likely to shake you out of any rut you may find yourself in. Growth and expansion in a favored pursuit such as numerology, astrology, or science fiction can be made now since the desire for learning is enhanced. Luck through games of chance could bring a small boost to the coffers.

Sunday the 6th. A compulsion to satisfy your needs and desires can bring relationship issues to a head. Communicating with your partner exactly how you are feeling can bring a deeper level of understanding. But you need to realize that it is not just your feelings that have to be addressed. Catching up on study or completing a homework assignment can put you ahead of the class now.

Weekly Summary

Most of this week and into the next you might experience difficulties in your love life. If you feel that you have been or are still riding an emotional roller coaster, these feelings are likely to continue for a little while longer. Keep in mind that the adverse planetary energy influencing your sign now is only temporary and will settle down.

If you are typical of your Sun sign, impetuosity as well as rash and unthinking behavior will emerge periodically. Be aware of these characteristics now, as you are still under a mild accident-prone influence until Mars, your impulsive ruler, moves away from an adverse aspect with Uranus, planet of unexpected situations. Don't be disappointed if someone who is usually reliable lets you down. Try to be more prepared if there is a next time.

There is bound to be drama when the Scorpio Full Moon spotlights your sector of secret deals and personal security. A partner or business associate could question the current state of a bank account, shared monies, or outstanding debts. Draw up a complete list of expected income and expenses. Still, this isn't the best time to be drawn into financial discussions. Emotions may be too close to the surface for rational discourse.

19th Week/May 7–13

Monday the 7th. There are times when you need to stop, look, and listen to what others say, and today may be one of those times. Financial commitments that you cannot easily get out of should be put on hold. Wait a few more days before setting plans in concrete, as you may have a change of mind. Pass on knowledge to those who can gain from your wisdom and special expertise.

Tuesday the 8th. Venus settles into Cancer today, highlighting the home and family sector of your solar chart. Appreciation for your possessions brings a desire to make living conditions more comfortable and visually pleasing. Even the most outgoing among you are likely to prefer socializing and entertaining at home with friends rather than going out on the town.

Wednesday the 9th. An urge to have more freedom to explore new and unconventional ideas and plans can bring on feelings of discontentment or restlessness. Personal insecurities could also be a problem, as physical vim and vigor are currently at low ebb. Pressure surrounding finances may be exerted if you have not handled your money efficiently in the recent past.

Thursday the 10th. A potential scandal may be looming for someone close. If revealing information does come to light, show your true colors and stand by the person who could be under siege. Be careful with body language and what you say aloud. Others could misconstrue actions and words. Avoid driving yourself to the limit. Take a break and rest, especially after work.

Friday the 11th. Messenger Mercury zooms into versatile Gemini, highlighting your sector of communication. You may spend more time on the phone, e-mail, or instant messaging over the next three weeks. Curiosity will increase, as will boredom, if your mind is not continually stimulated. Reaching out to communicate with the public by presenting lectures or seminars brings positive results.

Saturday the 12th. Rest, relaxation, or even solitude could appeal if you have had a busy working week. You may not want to conform to your usual activities or routine chores. If you feel you are in rut, take off for a drive, stroll downtown, or spend an extra hour in bed. If staying home is your preference, just try to focus on mundane tasks that do not require a lot of energy and thought.

Sunday the 13th. Aries eyes are firmly set on personal goals and ambitions. With increased physical resources at your disposal, this is the time to begin new activities or make desired changes. Now that you can see the chance to realize your goals, you are able to forge ahead without allowing anything to stand in your way. Relationships on the home front may become problematic as issues around power and control emerge.

Weekly Summary

Career, love, and money are some of the areas affected by the current planetary trends. A continued need to keep a check on your expenditures remains. However, you should be capable of managing your money more efficiently as well as stretching available funds far enough to cover outstanding bills.

Take care when dealing with authority figures, and don't make assumptions. Go that extra distance and polish up your tact and diplomacy skills to avoid rubbing others the wrong way. Some strong stabilizing influences surround you. But this is not the most opportune period to consider a new business venture or large transaction, especially if this involves taking some type of risk.

Be clear and concise when issuing instructions to children, employees, or others in your inner circle. Communications are prone to mix-ups and confusion. Venus travels into Cancer, accentuating home and family interests as well as urging lively changes in the domestic sphere. Unattached Aries should experience success looking for love and romance much closer to home.

20th Week/May 14–20

Monday the 14th. You are in your element today as the Aries Moon accents your first house of personality. Taking control of family affairs or a gala social gathering will test patience and resilience. But you will revel in the challenge this presents. Meeting a deadline may not happen, so slow down and do the job more efficiently. What doesn't get finished today can be completed tomorrow.

Tuesday the 15th. Regardless of how physically fit you are, you can expect an increased boost of energy now. Your ruler, dynamo Mars, has entered your sign of Aries in your first house of self and personal interests. Self-motivation and the courage to chase your goals are heightened, as well as your ambitions and ego. One drawback is that you may not look before you leap. You could be guilty of jumping to incorrect conclusions.

Wednesday the 16th. An up-and-down day for Aries. If you have goods to return to a store for a credit refund, try not to go during the morning hours. Disputes with sales staff or a manager are more likely, plus you may not receive your money back. Wait until later in the day when the Taurus New Moon heralds a productive period for your personal finances and income.

Thursday the 17th. Restlessness may urge you to travel short distances to experience a change of environment. Even running errands could be exciting, especially if they involve localities never visited before. Business-oriented Aries should have a successful day if involved in negotiating a contract or deal. This is also a suitable time to seek a pay increase.

Friday the 18th. Resist the urge to engage in idle chatter. Although this may be a pleasant way to socialize, the time spent could be better utilized in a more worthwhile and productive pursuit. Also there will be less chance of saying the wrong thing or being caught by the boss. You could act erratically, experience a sudden infatuation, or feel that you want to break out of a perceived rut.

Saturday the 19th. With patience in short supply, steer clear of loved ones until any aggressive tendencies have disappeared. Early morning is the time when your temper is likely to be quickly aroused. Time spent in the garden or on a long hike should be restorative and help quell anger-making issues. By early evening romantic feelings return, and you should be ready to participate in fun times with a loved one.

Sunday the 20th. The desire for greater freedom may be evident as restlessness and impatience for something to happen are strong. Creative ideas can easily be translated into action. With mental energy stimulated, you will be eager to participate in intellectual pursuits rather than physical activities. Be careful if discussing controversial topics. You could be tactless if you don't like what is conveyed.

Weekly Summary

Ambitions and desires are aroused as energizer Mars challenges mighty Pluto. Physical stamina may seem to be higher, which could urge you to overwork and try to do too much, even to the point of exhaustion. Use your energy wisely. Slow down, rest when you need to. Goals set in place for the week can be achieved if you proceed at a steady pace.

Aries working or traveling overseas need to apply caution with your personal safety. It is not the best time to set off for places unknown or to explore areas that are considered global danger spots. Confidential matters could be revealed, bringing embarrassment for Aries. Take a proactive stance, and let those who should be aware of your secrets know in advance.

The Taurus New Moon could mark the inception of a new financial endeavor in which you combine energies with another to bring mutual gains. With your ruler Mars in your sign now, your confidence and enthusiasm will soar. To get the best results from a situation, utilize this positive influence by being resourceful, initiating projects as well as completing waiting tasks.

21st Week/May 21–27

Monday the 21st. Today the Sun joins Mercury in Gemini, your third house of communication, neighborhood affairs, and educational advancement. A business meeting, conference, or study-group discussion should proceed without a hitch as well as bring productive results. Make sure you record all relevant information. You could overlook or forget something that is important if you rely on memory alone.

Tuesday the 22nd. Social plans are likely to unravel at the last minute. If you are keen to socialize this evening, have an alternate plan in the pipeline so you are not all dressed up with nowhere to go. Feelings of anger could arise because of the expectations of others. If you choose the right time to speak up and explain your concerns, a satisfactory resolution should be found fairly quickly.

Wednesday the 23rd. Patience might be severely lacking for you again today. This could concern a frustrating situation or issue as well as annoyance with others. Differences of opinion with coworkers or an employer could arise because you feel current working conditions are not up to your standards. You are full of inspirational ideas and creative plans but will need to double-check that these are realistic.

Thursday the 24th. Be careful concerning details for an employment project. Something could backfire, leaving someone with egg on his or her face. Make sure it is not you or that you shoulder any blame. If you want to feel great, improve your zest to enjoy life more and look at your healthiest best. Now is the time to drink more water and combine plenty of fresh fruit and vegetables with your normal diet.

Friday the 25th. Beware any propensity to go to extremes, to overreact, or to try and bend others to your way of thinking. Issues with those around you are likely to arise if you come on too strong and try bully-boy tactics. You need excitement and a variety of diversions but not at the expense of others. Singles meeting a romantic possibility could be in for a fun time but perhaps not a long time.

Saturday the 26th. A public relations event or meeting should proceed smoothly this morning. A date with a business partner or associate for a breakfast meeting may be canceled or delayed. Opportunities for friendship or love could arise for the unattached. Aries in a committed relationship could be frustrated if you feel you are giving more than you are receiving.

Sunday the 27th. Although you could experience discord with or opposition from others, this may be a good time to speak up. Old grievances not resolved can surface for an airing. If socializing with casual friends, try to avoid gossip, innuendo, or intrigue. Others may judge you on your ability to remain cool and noncommittal. A novel or movie featuring conspiracy and mystery could appeal as a way to unwind.

Weekly Summary

Things get busy with the Sun visiting Gemini from now until June 21. As an already active and on-the-go Aries, you could find the tempo of life moving up another notch. An urge to see and do more can find you taking off on impromptu journeys to sightsee, visit friends out of town, or shop away from your usual stores.

A keen interest in novel and progressive ideas can provide the opportunity to do something different and give variety to your work and daily existence. Singles can find excitement in romance providing you are seeking fun and diversity and not a deep and meaningful love affair. Expect social plans, appointments, and meetings to be canceled or altered at the last minute.

You could feel frazzled by the pressure of constantly being on the move. Try to keep cool and calm. Relieve stress by engaging in activities that relax both body and mind. An art exhibition, the theater, a rock concert, or sports might appeal as a way to block personal and business matters that continually invade your thoughts.

22nd Week/May 28–June 3

Monday the 28th. Participating in artistic projects can give your imagination the chance to blossom today. With support and encouragement from others, you realize you are on the right track. Treat romantic encounters carefully, as you may be deceived by your own emotions. Avoid a tendency to view a potential love through rose-colored glasses, or worse still, place the person on a pedestal.

Tuesday the 29th. Not knowing exactly how much money is required for a commitment, purchase, or deal could be a source of agitation. Chill out, Aries, all will be revealed fairly soon and to your satisfaction. Communicative Mercury is now visiting Cancer, your sector of family and domestic concerns. The home environment will be a focus of many discussions and decisions about desired living arrangements.

Wednesday the 30th. Important money matters or circumstances relating to joint finances, taxes, or insurance coverage may require attention now. Stand up for your rights if you get the runaround with an insurance claim. Increased bickering and backbiting among those who share your domestic life are likely. Make sure that you are not the one who instigates this behavior. It will come back to haunt you.

Thursday the 31st. You are in the mood for action today. The Full Moon in expansive Sagittarius conveys an urge to pursue philosophical or intellectual endeavors. A lecture, workshop, or training course could appeal to increase your knowledge or employment skills. Settling a family disagreement may be more difficult than usual, as emotions are likely to be running high. Use tact and diplomacy, and discord will dissipate much quicker.

Friday June 1st. Dreams may be an inspiration for the artistically inclined. With organizational skills enhanced, the talent and know-how to implement creative projects and get your plans off the ground are evident. Attend group gatherings and push your personal interests and ambitions. Bringing others around to your way of thinking in an unobtrusive manner assists your cause.

Saturday the 2nd. It is time to think about getting away for a well-deserved break. Your travel agent is sure to have great ideas on the best current deals. If the bank balance can't sustain an expensive trip, learning more about the customs and traditions of faraway destinations may have to suffice until funds permit. Treat your mate to dinner and indulge in a meal that is a cultural treat for the taste buds.

Sunday the 3rd. Study long-term goals and make the necessary changes to suit your current circumstances. You may not see an immediate improvement, but later you can reap the financial benefits. You could realize that you have reached a point where you know you have taken on too much. Seek support and assistance from others if you feel that too many responsibilities have been thrust upon you.

Weekly Summary

Energy levels, self-confidence, and an enterprising spirit remain high. Don't let feelings of guilt stop you from enjoying activities outside of home and work, as you do need to play as well. Mobile Mercury shifts gears now, joining Venus in home-loving Cancer. Domestic activities and home concerns are emphasized. A move is strongly indicated for Rams.

Rethink ideas and plans, especially those whose progress you are no longer happy or comfortable with. A welcome new addition to the family or guests coming for an extended stay may prompt an urgent reshuffle.

Removing clutter and changing the home surroundings can provide extra space for living.

Utilize the energy of the Sagittarius Full Moon to bring the successful culmination of a special project or endeavor. Being on the receiving end of some harsh words or comments could urge you to stand up for your rights. If you believe that your views and opinions should be considered by others, discuss this honestly and without drama or emotional displays.

23rd Week/June 4–10

Monday the 4th. Positive and constructive action can occur today as your ruler Mars adds fuel to the ambitions of expansive Jupiter. Self-confidence begins to soar. Jump to initiate changes to goals and personal desires. Prospects for a successful outcome are enhanced, providing realism merges with your current aspirations. Some good luck brings a welcome boost to depleted funds.

Tuesday the 5th. Apply caution in your dealings with others. Arguments involving neighbors or in-laws may erupt into a nasty war of words. Venus, lusty goddess of the zodiac, glides into regal Leo and will accentuate pleasure and leisure activities over the next few weeks. Pursuing love, fun, and entertainment will be the ticket to experience joy and contentment.

Wednesday the 6th. Don't allow worries to upset your equilibrium this morning. Revelations that come to light may need to be viewed from a different perspective. Put your trust in those who have been of assistance in the past. A social gathering that has business overtones may bring a new romantic spark. Engaging in lighthearted discourse could reveal that you both have common interests that can strengthen a bond.

Thursday the 7th. Sleep could be disturbed by strange dreams bringing anxieties. By seeking answers to these hidden messages, a wonderland of solutions could open up. An emotional need for fulfillment could be productively expressed by performing charitable or volunteer work at your local hospice or center for the elderly. Past good works may find you featured in your community newspaper.

Friday the 8th. It may be time to examine feelings, current behavior, and attitudes. Put aside doubts about what might have been. Concentrate on what is happening right now since you cannot change past actions or conduct. Socializing with others will seem like a chore for much of the day. Lock yourself away with a good book or a DVD if you cannot be bothered entertaining guests this evening.

Saturday the 9th. Special plans bring excited anticipation now. The problem will come if your ideas are not based on reality and are just fantasies of your fertile imagination. An excess of nervous energy can have you running around frantically trying to complete household chores or errands. Much more will be accomplished if you slow down and focus on one particular task at a time.

Sunday the 10th. A day to enjoy your local surroundings can include a stroll around the park with a lover, a trip to the beach with youngsters, or a chat with friends at the local coffee shop. If it's sunny, include a good moisturizer and sunscreen to protect your skin. Overall health is also protected by ensuring your diet contains good amounts of fruit, vegetables, and whole-wheat grains.

Weekly Summary

Your ruler Mars features strongly, working in tandem with beneficent Jupiter. You will find a new way to fulfill your goals. Lots of ideas are whizzing around in your head. Study and travel are highlights. A broadening of options is foreseen. A magic moment comes when you pass an examination or receive an honor.

Taking an artistic risk could bring recognition for your skills and expertise. Vixen Venus in lively Leo emphasizes your creative sector. Love, laughter, and entertainment are promised. If there is a choice between work and play, you will prefer to have a good time. Balancing recreation with regular obligations will become a juggling act.

The trends toward love and romance are starred now, and socially you will be in demand. It is time to update your wardrobe, check out the range of beauty products available, and schedule an appointment for the new hairstylist your friends have been raving about. Steadily going through the routine of daily life and work responsibilities can seem boring, so you will be looking for fun.

24th Week/June 11–17

Monday the 11th. Spending time observing those around you could provide the answers as to why some people act the way they do. Having this information could prove to be beneficial later on. Recent setbacks with finances may have resulted in more caution applied to fiscal management. Purchasing a few treats now is unlikely to dent the budget. But don't get too carried away or all your good intentions will be lost.

Tuesday the 12th. Although you may welcome an increase in income, remember the more work you take on the less time you have for yourself and family. Set your priorities now, giving due consideration to other areas of your life. There is only yourself to blame if you cross your boundaries and become overloaded. Take a break from the social whirl. You may have been overdoing it and are now in need of rest and relaxation.

Wednesday the 13th. Vision and opportunity are harmonizing now, making this a time of advancement. Take advantage so that inspiration and imagination can transport you into realms of fantasy. You will love shopping for bright new clothes. Colorful accessories will be the perfect panacea if you feel your current wardrobe is out of date or suffering from a bad case of dowdiness.

Thursday the 14th. The Gemini New Moon impacts your sector of short trips and communication. So it is a favorable time to organize a vacation or take a short break. Devotion to studies and writing should be rewarded. When Mercury goes reverse tomorrow, in-depth research will be favored. Take an active part in business meetings and discussion groups. Others will notice your excellent communication skills.

Friday the 15th. Mercury, trickster of the zodiac, goes retrograde, conveying a possible array of circumstances beyond your control. From now until July 9, be more careful when speaking to those with whom you live. Messages are likely to end up being delayed, garbled, or they may not make it to the right person. This planetary influence is not all unpleasant. It is an excellent period to renegotiate previous property leases or deals.

Saturday the 16th. Planning the next home renovation or beautifying your environment involves a burst of creative energy. Make sure this does not become a larger undertaking than expected or budgeted for. Entertain guests this evening in the comfort of your own home. Showcase your newly acquired culinary skills by whipping up a menu that everyone will talk about for weeks to come.

Sunday the 17th. Don't be a martyr. Ask family to assist with the backlog of household tasks. Several pairs of hands are quicker than two. Powers of concentration are strong, creating the right atmosphere to begin a new project requiring a special creative touch. News from a distance may involve children or a pregnancy. Consider arranging a surprise visit to catch up with someone close who is currently living far away.

Weekly Summary

Ultraefficiency and practicality can be applied to both your work and personal life now. There is a very good chance of achieving whatever you set out to do, but remember to include plenty of family and leisure time in your plans. Better trends for finances also beckon. However, care and attention should be applied, particularly if you have been a little lax and ignoring money matters lately.

Great new ideas come easier with the influences of the New Moon in Gemini. Don't let your creative energies go to waste, but put plans into action and watch for a successful outcome. If you want to make things happen, give it your best shot now. Implement new plans and projects prior to the Mercury retrograde period, which might cause delays and hiccups.

From now until July 9, finish projects around the house that have been started but not completed. It is also time to clear the clutter by going through your basement, attic, and drawers. Donate, sell, have a garage sale, or throw away junk you no longer need. Rest, relax, and spend time at home with your favorite people.

25th Week/June 18–24

Monday the 18th. It's an easy choice to take a gamble, but it's harder to make up something that has been lost. Stay clear of the gaming tables, and keep your money safely ensconced in your wallet. Take extra precautions with your personal safety now, especially if you are usually a laid-back and carefree Ram. Avoid areas where criminal activity is rife, and make sure you are accompanied by another if venturing out after dark.

Tuesday the 19th. Lady Luck is smiling sweetly in matters of finances. If investments are set up carefully and correctly, you will move one step closer to securing your future security. However, your love life might not run as smoothly. It may be tempting to take a superficial approach to relationship issues that demand a more in-depth understanding of any current difficulties.

Wednesday the 20th. Keep your eyes and ears open. A lot could be gleaned by watching a superior, giving you the jump on the competition. Now is an excellent time to begin a health and fitness program. Hard work and effort will pay off with increased physical strength and more energy to pursue the activities you love. Don't allow others to interfere with your daily duties and responsibilities. Be especially aware of a busybody coworker or annoying relative.

Thursday the 21st. Tread lightly if exploring new territories on the job. At midday the Sun enters Cancer, bringing attention to family relationships for the next month. Renovations and refurbishing domestic conditions could occupy much of your time. Do your homework first if you are looking at major modifications, and check out the prior work of service people before accepting quotations.

Friday the 22nd. Someone could be showing signs of jealously toward you. If it is a business associate it would be better to ignore them. At least you know that you must be doing something right, so continue in the same vein. Uranus, planet of chaos, will start to go retrograde now and may bring on a brief period of impatience with rules and regulations. Stay focused on group aims and this will soon pass.

Saturday the 23rd. Tensions in relationships are likely to rise to the surface. If a particular issue has been troubling you, this could now come to a head. There is no point pretending that everything is fine if it isn't. Face facts and take action to restore domestic harmony. A project or business idea that is in a developmental phase may need more of your attention. Problems with red tape could cause frustrating delays.

Sunday the 24th. Your ruler Mars now visits Taurus and your financial sector. It is time to turn your attention to money management and strategies. Serious consideration about what you want to do with your money can bring a more efficient accountability of expenses. Facing challenges connected with career and earning potential will be easier now since your motivation to improve income and personal finances is higher.

Weekly Summary

Relationship issues can be a source of angst. Staying connected to your partner may be difficult. Take the time to look seriously at your love life concerning your attitude to emotional responsibilities. Positive improvements can be made if you do. Trying harder to appreciate the difference between your personality and interests and those of your partner could be a starting point.

You can strike the right balance between optimism and reality when it comes to your finances. With luck on your side, this is an excellent period to make your money work for you. Take a chance, if necessary, but avoid anything too risky. Put spare funds into a rock-solid investment that should bring future dividends.

A new health interest or participation in a physical activity will appeal. Home or garden may receive the benefit of your renewed energy. Mars in Taurus will energize your earning potential, pushing along matters concerning possessions and finances. You could become aware of a new source of income, or you may receive an unexpected offer too good to refuse.

26th Week/June 25–July 1

Monday the 25th. Pay off your debts first if you have cash to spare. Even though it may be tempting to purchase a treat, maintaining a healthy credit rating is important for future progress. Don't underrate your abilities or you can undermine your self-confidence, thus encouraging a self-fulfilling prophecy. Remaining optimistic may be difficult but is a challenge you need to face today.

Tuesday the 26th. Something hidden or confidential may need to be dealt with and resolved whether you like it or not. You may be inclined to devote time and money into making your environment safe and secure. A financial investment in something you love and value will prove to be beneficial in the long term. Paintings or art objects should be especially appealing.

Wednesday the 27th. It could be time to get out and discover places you have never seen before. Arrange a long weekend and pick somewhere close by to visit, where you can shop, wander around, and lap up the local atmosphere. Better than expected examination results will have you in a buzz. And so will the delivery of a new vehicle if you have an exploratory spirit!

Thursday the 28th. What begins as a heated discussion could get to the core of matters, with positive resolutions. Getting issues off your chest can also clear the air and further your insight into the idiosyncrasies of others. A new commercial venture looks promising. Plans can be formulated to move ahead next month. Finish business activities early so you can put romance on the agenda this evening.

Friday the 29th. Limitations may seem unreasonably hard to bear right now. Endeavoring to stay cool and calm may be difficult but not impossible if you make an extra effort. Apply caution when dealing with sharp edges, especially if you are working in areas with poor lighting. If you have been experiencing negativity in your relationship, this should begin to clear up. Give love a helping hand and arrange a romantic dinner for two.

Saturday the 30th. Muster all your energies. Steer clear of sensitive, touchy others. Instead, use the influence of the Capricorn Full Moon in a positive manner to bring outstanding tasks to fruition. Singles, your heart and mind may not be in sync when a romantic potential comes along. You don't need to decide whether to commit to a new relationship now. Waiting will give you the chance to consider all the options.

Sunday July 1st. Use excess energy and enthusiasm to your best advantage. Your creativity is also running hot. Look through magazines and department stores for the inspiration to turn your home-decorating plans into a showcase that will be the envy of your friends. A no-nonsense approach to life is needed to help resolve relationship issues. Singles, love is not something that will happen spontaneously. You have to look for it.

Weekly Summary

Exercising the brain could mean signing up for an educational course or an informal class on an interesting topic. Making exciting plans to visit a faraway friend or thinking about destinations for your next vacation will be something to look forward to whenever you need cheering up this week. Spending time with someone who makes you laugh is also likely to make a difference in your mood.

Be careful with spending if you have implemented a self-imposed economy drive. This week you could easily throw away more money than you should on spur-of-the-moment purchases. Misunderstandings are likely to occur with your lover and might quickly erupt into a full-blown argument. It could become increasingly difficult to resolve the conflict unless common sense prevails.

Emotions that get stirred up may not feel very comfortable. Blame it on the Full Moon. People are likely to be extrasensitive, could easily take offense, and climb on their high horse over something you say or do. Avoid topics that you know are unduly controversial and likely to increase tension.

27th Week/July 2–8

Monday the 2nd. Keeping a financial promise you made in a rash moment may mean handing over some of your hard-earned cash to a friend in need. Only lend enough to ease financial pressure, and make sure you draw up a repayment plan. You don't want to be out of pocket too long. You will want others to show they love you. They do, but you may not have taken enough notice of affectionate displays.

Tuesday the 3rd. Old family business surfaces, providing the chance to discuss past hurts that can lead to resolution and healing. Once this has been sorted out, you can give yourself a pat on the back for all the good things achieved. A hobby could lead to extra income. Make the most of your skills and experiences by creating something that conveys pride in your achievements and adds to the bank account.

Wednesday the 4th. Exercise restraint with far-out ideas today. Don't be surprised if others are not as accepting of your plans as you had hoped. However, don't fall into the trap of inhibiting your creative expression. This Fourth of July is a good time to contact a friend who has been on your mind lately. Both of you will enjoy the holiday more by catching up on all the news. If children are involved in festivities, take care with fireworks.

Thursday the 5th. The urge to nurture and take care of others could spill over into taking on charitable work that involves looking after those in need. Use humor to overcome issues with others. Emotions could become exposed as you bear the brunt of a friend's or colleague's ill temper. Endeavor to remain cool and calm and find your own personal space. Do what would make you the happiest. Pamper yourself tonight.

Friday the 6th. Asserting your independence is food for the soul. But do it with tact and diplomacy. The Aries Moon in your personality zone begins a new monthly cycle. This period can increase your drive for personal freedom as you search for ways to become more efficient at the activities or hobbies you enjoy. Release any attachment to plans and ideas if the combination of forces is working against the desired outcome.

Saturday the 7th. Singles, romantic encounters increase if you open up. Existing relationships are likely to be active, exciting, and romantically inclined. Impatience with continually accommodating the whims of others could impel you to do whatever takes your fancy instead of worrying about the needs of others. If you have the day off, take time to indulge and pamper yourself. Have a facial or massage and get set for a big night out.

Sunday the 8th. Love and romance rule. So create the right ambience and take advantage of the passionate advances of your lover or spouse. Plan a dreamy getaway for two, and schedule through the Internet to get the best deals. Singles won't be immune to love either. A possible candidate could be someone from another country who makes your heart beat faster. It could be love at first sight.

Weekly Summary

Your love life comes into considerable focus and attention. Anxiety around where your relationship is headed increases nervousness as well as frustration. Stay detached, and you will be able to see things in a clearer light. Now is a turning point, with opportunities for marriage or the potential for separation and divorce.

There may be periods when you wish that people would just disappear and leave you alone. If they don't, they may be sorry. Suffering fools gladly is not something Aries excels at and especially right now. Take advantage of time alone to do your own thing. A chance to catch up on unfinished work or to correct a past mistake may be presented.

By week's end expect a healthy and passionate dose of romance. Sexual tensions are sparked. Singles can experience a powerful time to reignite an old flame who has returned from overseas. Fun and enjoyment can be experienced with reunions of old friends, family gatherings, and socializing with coworkers. Expect a smattering of intense moments to arise that could be fun or even extreme.

28th Week/July 9–15

Monday the 9th. Money could flow out of your bank account unless you have the willpower to stop the flood. Keeping away from your favorite shopping haunts will enable you to save rather than spend your cash. Tonight talkative Mercury progresses forward, which signals an end to any mix-ups that have been causing you so much angst and frustration around domestic matters.

Tuesday the 10th. Mix with neighbors whenever the occasion arises. You will enjoy catching up with the gossip and finding out what is happening. Even stopping for a quick chat or a cup of coffee will make you feel part of the community. Don't spoil your good rapport with others by putting your nose in the affairs of those who haven't asked for help.

Wednesday the 11th. Watch your communication with others. You may find that your words are being used against you. Impatience and restlessness strike today, urging you to do everything at double the normal rate. If you are traveling, an eagerness to arrive at your destination will cause irritation if you meet delays or hitches. Take a good book that you can really get into in case you have to suffer long delays.

Thursday the 12th. Today will see you busy running errands, visiting friends, surfing the Internet, and generally socializing with others. Seek information that can give you leverage on a financial level. Be prepared to compromise in negotiations. But be on guard for power plays as you could be caught up in the old battles of others. An unexpected development may require a quick shift in plans.

Friday the 13th. You will probably prefer to remain in familiar surroundings, enjoying the company of family and friends on this Friday the thirteenth. Not that the date concerns you. You want more rest and relaxation and not to do anything too energetic. Spending time improving home comforts, pottering in the garden, or embarking on a creative pursuit could appeal if you prefer activity to lounging on the couch or entertaining guests.

Saturday the 14th. There is a lot of movement on the home front now with today's Cancer New Moon preparing you for change. You may want to move to a locality that provides more opportunities for children. If you decide to stay where you are, changes will be made around your home. Even if alterations are not major, a more positive atmosphere with energy flowing will prevail.

Sunday the 15th. You should be pleased with the way things are going now. An opportunity exists to strengthen intimate or professional relationships that are working well and to sort out those that are not. If your love life fits into the latter category, your effort can turn things around, bringing rewards of a loving and supportive partnership. Socialize and you could make some worthwhile contacts.

Weekly Summary

Exciting possibilities open up now. Mercury goes into direct motion, supporting new ideas and resolutions to recent problems or delays. Caution with money is recommended. It will be easy for a highly skilled salesperson to convince you that you really do need a product when you know you don't.

Don't make promises you are unable to keep. Learn from past errors to prevent a repetition of more mistakes. Expect the unexpected midweek, and you will be prepared for anything that occurs. Keep your feet on the ground and realize more chances to impress a boss or other authority figure. If you go overboard, you run the risk of scattering your energies.

At week's end it would be beneficial to spend more time at home. The need to address domestic conditions is likely to arise. But you will know how to handle any problems. If it is possible or practical, working from home could help to resolve some of your problems. Review issues around independence or dependency in relationships.

29th Week/July 16–22

Monday the 16th. Put your affairs in order to ensure that long-range goals and financial security will meet your later needs. Break away from responsibilities for a few hours. It is time to focus on a creative pastime through which you can do your own thing and have lots of fun at the same time. Be more realistic regarding a romantic relationship and let go of fantasy.

Tuesday the 17th. Be careful of promises made today, as good intentions could backfire. In your eagerness to impress the right people, you might overlook the increased work you have let yourself in for. Children may be a source of difficulty for parents and probably need a firmer hand. There is no end to what may need to be done, but you probably won't have the time to let trivial matters become overwhelming.

Wednesday the 18th. Things could quickly spiral out of control if you let your ego get in the way. Remain open-minded to the thoughts and views of others. Even though you have strong opinions of your own, wisdom lies in the words offered by others. Stay on course with work, apply effort, and you will get the positive results you are hoping for.

Thursday the 19th. Don't try to fit everything you need to do into today's agenda. It will only cause tension with others, and you will end up cranky and tired. Share plans and ideas with those who can be helpful in getting the ball rolling. Be enthusiastic and positive but also remain realistic. Making promises you cannot keep or deliver on time may end up being expensive and damaging to your reputation.

Friday the 20th. Daydreaming will enhance your imagination, but it is not the best time to make important plans or decisions. You may be susceptible to the suggestions of others now, so wait until your head is clearer. The evening is an opportune time to get together with friends for an activity you haven't been involved in for a while. You may receive unexpected but favorable news concerning an application for a course of study.

Saturday the 21st. You will be more in tune with emotions today. It is an ideal time for sorting out problems that have sprung up with friends or business associates. Lately, others may be expressing their intentions but acting entirely differently. Although you know you are appreciated, the people in your life may be remiss in telling you so. Voice your needs and receive the admiration you deserve.

Sunday the 22nd. Getting on with others, especially if they are older, should be very easy. Your affable nature can smooth ruffled feathers and make everyone else feel comfortable and at ease. You may not be in the mood for energetic socializing, preferring more low-key activities. An inclination to shop until you drop may not be shared by a partner, so go easy with the credit card.

Weekly Summary

Concentrating totally on practical matters might prove difficult. Change your patterns, habits, or do something physical whenever restlessness emerges. Dance, play a sport, or go for a walk to avert boredom. If energy is channeled wisely, you can focus and avoid frivolous distractions. You may support the efforts of children to move toward independence.

Maintain your honesty and integrity in all your dealings. Good vibes for work exist now, with a promotion or better employment conditions offered. Although not known for your sensitivity, this week finds you more receptive to the emotions of others. This attitude can help you cooperate with others. Don't overcommit or promise too much. You will feel foolish if you overextend and cannot cope with an increased workload.

Look after yourself as well as others. Take the time to feed your body with essential nourishment. Throw away, or at least reduce, your consumption of coffee, cigarettes, and rich desserts. Saying no when others make unreasonable requests is something that usually gives you problems. Remember this when others try to take advantage or take your friendship too much for granted.

30th Week/July 23–29

Monday the 23rd. You are now in a lucky cycle. Follow your instincts and benefits will come. The Sun in Leo will see your social life pick up between now and August 23. Take a good look at finances, especially with insurance and taxes. You could discover that you are paying more than you should. Creativity flourishes when you think outside the box.

Tuesday the 24th. Time spent with loved ones and those who share your views and beliefs can be encouraging. It is important to keep your feet firmly on the ground, especially where money and friendships are involved.

Lending funds to others or spending for the sake of it might feel good at the time, but you will have to pay for your indulgence sooner or later when the bills arrive.

Wednesday the 25th. You could have the impression that someone disapproves of you or your actions. It may not be pleasant to know that others are not thinking highly of you, but try not to let this get you down. They are entitled to their opinions, and you know their evaluation is wrong. Planning a vacation to an intriguing destination helps to put any negativity out of your mind.

Thursday the 26th. If a relationship is changing, this is an excellent opportunity to discuss your feelings with your partner. Resist the temptation to insist that your way is the right way. It takes two to maintain and make a relationship work. A surprise invitation this evening could turn into a pleasant gathering that helps a budding friendship or love affair to blossom further.

Friday the 27th. Promote your best attributes to those who count. If your romantic plans have been at a standstill, you could discover the reason now, with lovely Venus backtracking in the sky. Perhaps these setbacks are a disguised blessing as you take time to review what you require in an intimate relationship. You are in the mood to relax and enjoy the harmonious vibes of family and friends this evening.

Saturday the 28th. People will be quick to respond to you. Don't be afraid to raise unusual ideas. Expect positive results from these proposals. Almost no subject will be too difficult for you to grasp if you are determined to comprehend and learn. Seek fun and enjoyment with a stimulating group of friends. The constant bantering and pleasant atmosphere will be invigorating.

Sunday the 29th. Good things happen suddenly and unexpectedly today. This may mean rethinking your schedule, which might not thrill you. Go with the flow. Long-term gains make it worth the effort. The Full Moon in Aquarius contributes to tension among those in your friendship circle. Be on guard, and don't take sides if an argument occurs between friends.

Weekly Summary

Party time begins for Aries now that the Sun is visiting the royal sign of Leo in your love and amusement sector. Existing love relationships are benefited through warmth and happiness. Singles may have the chance to mix business with pleasure and possibly meet a suitable romantic partner at the same time. Take advantage of this period to allow creative skills to reach a new level.

Midweek could find your energy levels below par. Arrange a summer vacation if it has been awhile since you had time off. If you are not heading off for a break, you may be thinking about foreign ventures. Learning the basics of another language to enhance employment chances or to communicate with prospective clients could be an exciting challenge you will enjoy.

The Full Moon in quirky Aquarius urges you to catch up with friends you have been neglecting. Ring or e-mail those who live too far away for personal contact to keep the bonds strong. Don't forget to pamper loved ones. Buy a small gift or flowers to show that their support is appreciated.

31st Week/July 30–August 5

Monday the 30th. If you have a busy day ahead, you will need to be organized and disciplined. Otherwise, accomplishments and productivity will be only slightly above zero. You may find you want to daydream, paint, fantasize, or do anything other than perform daily tasks waiting for action. Take a friend as a navigator or use a road map if traveling.

Tuesday the 31st. Attention is drawn toward your personal finances or lack thereof. Listen to the advice of friends who see the warning signs of a current bad attitude toward love, money, and your spending habits. Be open to new ways of finding amusements that are cost efficient. Children or a lover might need more pampering. Put aside your own needs and administer some tender loving care.

Wednesday August 1st. You may feel that all you want is to be alone. Events could get under your skin, bringing on tension and anxiety. Don't brood about issues. Otherwise, a headache is likely to result in great discomfort. If financial stress is causing angst, the best advice is to avoid shops and advertisements. You have a choice in your working environment, so seek privacy and your own space.

Thursday the 2nd. It's time for self-indulgence, especially if you have been working nonstop. Purchase a book or CD that sets your mind thinking stress-free thoughts and relaxes your body and soul. If you are lucky enough to have the day off, spend quality time with loved ones, including the little ones in your family. Tonight find someone expert in the art of massage, put your feet up, and enjoy the moment.

Friday the 3rd. With the Moon in Aries, the day will pass with few issues or irritations other than a display of minor impatience or hasty action. If you have been working hard, rewards for efforts should now start to flow. Prepare yourself to look your best. Shop for a new outfit, visit a beauty salon, trim up the waistline, and you may be amazed how this works wonders on yourself and others.

Saturday the 4th. You'll be interested in your personal affairs and doing what you enjoy best. Be careful that all discussions don't revolve around you. Otherwise, someone is likely to object rather strongly. Practice wearing your smile, and you and everyone around you will be happier. As Mercury visits Leo from now until August

19, you are more inclined to engage in stimulating games and activities.

Sunday the 5th. Picnics, short drives, or an excursion to the beach would be a pleasant way to spend the day. Pack the refreshments and organize plenty of activities to keep the kids amused. Don't forget hats and sunscreen if the sun is blazing. A romantic issue could be making you feel vulnerable. Confide in someone you trust and receive valuable advice and assistance.

Weekly Summary

Money, money, and more money is the cry as this week begins. Unfortunately it seems that more will flow out of the coffers than in. Your head is likely to be spinning with incoming bills for children's expenses, special excursions, insurance accounts, and motor vehicle expenses. Don't allow guilty feelings to get in the way of implementing necessary cuts to the household budget.

By midweek, apart from finances, other issues will be mostly resolved. The constant frown you have been wearing disappears, to be replaced by a sunny smile. This is the time to update your looks. A new hairstyle, wardrobe, or beauty routine can make you feel renewed and glamorous. Don't be afraid to speak your mind, but do it gently.

Intellectual Mercury in Leo taps your zone of pleasure, leisure, and romance. Activities requiring creative input are favored. Exercise your brain, find mentally stimulating pursuits to occupy free time. Play games with youngsters that challenge mental alacrity and logic. Singles, be warned against playing mind games with a dating partner.

32nd Week/August 6–12

Monday the 6th. The threat of financial difficulties becomes obvious on some occasions, and this may be one.

Perhaps it is time to take a more responsible and self-controlled attitude if you are struggling to meet current commitments. If you are feeling tense, put on a meditation CD, turn off your mind, and relax. Tending the garden could appeal to Aries wanting to commune with nature in a practical manner.

Tuesday the 7th. Your mind may be racing today. It's a good idea to write down all the bright ideas that come flooding in. Otherwise, they could quickly disappear, leaving you wondering why you didn't record the flashes of inspiration. Paying attention to details is never your idea of fun. If the basics are ignored at work, errors are likely to occur requiring repeating tasks all over again.

Wednesday the 8th. Prepare for busy times ahead with your ruler Mars firmly ensconced in Gemini. The universe is sending a boost of energy to assist in the successful completion of projects and the motivation to press on with your plans. Through community activities, you can join with others to make a difference in your neighborhood. Last-minute arrangements could require your attention, but you will be glad to see to them.

Thursday the 9th. You have moved into a creative phase now. Skills and talents can be positively expressed through writing, painting, or music. This is a good time to get started on the poetry book or romance novel that has been on your mind for some time now. If your manuscript is complete, send it off to the publisher. There is a very good chance it will be accepted.

Friday the 10th. Practice deep breathing to remain calm. Domestic obligations are likely to feel burdensome, but common sense can resolve issues. Communications may be strained. If you are in a committed union, welcome the chance to discuss controversial topics. Even if you don't agree with your partner, you may learn something that excites you or provides a different slant on an age-old problem.

Saturday the 11th. Activities or pursuits that engage your adventurous side attract Rams today. A skiing weekend might appeal to the energetic. Or you might prefer to be a spectator rather than a participant in a team sport. Either way the fresh air will do you a world of good. A minor stroke of good fortune might enlarge your wallet. Romance is on the horizon for the young, and the not so young.

Sunday the 12th. A delightful day is ahead, with the Leo New Moon accenting your pleasure zone. Plan an adventure trip with your lover. If you have been hoping for a romantic getaway, this is the day to plan it. A playful mood can lead to lighthearted games either indoors or outdoors. Whatever takes your fancy works for you now. If you are nearing the delivery of a child, be prepared, as the birth could be imminent.

Weekly Summary

Find practical ways to release tension. If you know how to meditate or practice yoga, include these disciplines in your daily schedule. If you don't know these or other forms of relaxation techniques, perhaps it is time to learn. Warrior Mars enters Gemini in your information sector, bringing tempers to the boil quickly. Keep this in mind. Otherwise, disagreements and spats could spiral out of control.

Accomplishments are made by joining forces with neighbors, relatives, and those encountered on a daily basis. Now is a good time to promote your ideas and convince others of your abilities. Don't take offense if someone disagrees with your opinions. New relationships evolving may move to a new level.

Week's end signals a lucky time. A surge of optimism assists to clear obstacles standing in your way. Supported by a Leo New Moon, creative inspiration can help get new ventures off the ground. Aries journalists and foreign correspondents could have a scoop that will raise your profile as well as your earning capacity.

33rd Week/August 13–19

Monday the 13th. Your ability to create special experiences and environments for loved ones remains enhanced. Love goddess Venus brings a sense of permanency around relationships, which can lead to future happiness. You will prefer quiet candlelit dinners for two rather than noisy parties or gatherings. Tolerance for fussing by others will be at low ebb.

Tuesday the 14th. Restlessness abounds today. Mundane, almost tedious, tasks would be the most suitable occupation. Catch up on filing, data input, or uncomplicated household chores. You will enjoy the feeling of efficiency even if nothing major is completed. Throw away things you no longer need. Don't forget to recycle and help save the planet.

Wednesday the 15th. Turning on the charm wherever you go can be easy for Rams. You exude charisma and sensuality now. Any self-doubts about your popularity melt away as you work your magic on others. A travel agency beckons. Cultivate your desire to experience more out of life. Thumb through brochures of exotic destinations and begin plans for the trip of a lifetime.

Thursday the 16th. Don't fear change. At the same time, avoid rushing ahead without due care. A steady approach can steer you to the pathway of success. The magnetic effect you have on others will make demands on you socially. Others are likely to be in tune with your way of thinking. A creative interest arouses enthusiasm. Projects started now have a very good chance of going the distance.

Friday the 17th. Make room for spontaneity and flexibility in today's schedule. Intimate relationships are likely to intensify, with a deep compelling quality. Emotional feelings channeled into creative or artistic endeavors produce inspired work. Let others know exactly how you feel. Send an e-mail or write a love letter that expresses your true feelings.

Saturday the 18th. Take care of physical resources. A morning workout provides a healthy and energetic start to the weekend. Make sure that you also include a healthy breakfast to get you on your way. Discussions with a lover or friends may be essential now. You need to listen and learn from others now. Open up to an older or wiser person for helpful feedback if something is causing problems.

Sunday the 19th. Open your eyes and mind to the new day. Hop on a bus, train, or car and explore. Visit places of historical importance and expand your horizons. It would be a shame to spend the time alone. People will enjoy your company, so invite others to share the occasion. Students can spend time at the library researching topics that will add depth to homework or special assignments.

Weekly Summary

Confusion may arise for Rams. The main focus continues on your love zone, with conflicting planetary influences conveying complications. New loves that begin under these trends have the potential to endure. However, the possibility of deception exists in some relationships. Even though strong sexual desires could be present, proceed slowly in the romance stakes.

Concentration lapses make it difficult to focus on intricate details. Moves to impress the boss or a colleague could backfire. Let situations take a natural course. Pets are a source of unconditional love. However, ensure that the landlord approves before making any arrangements. Enjoyment means putting on the dancing shoes and having fun this week.

A display of aloofness or too serious behavior could keep others at a distance. Be affectionate and tell loved ones you care. Be careful that money is not frittered away on impulse if shopping for home-improvement items to enhance your living space. Think carefully about what adds appeal and value. Stick with quality and avoid trendy fads. They date quickly.

34th Week/August 20–26

Monday the 20th. A strong sense of responsibility focuses on loved ones. Offer moral support and let others know you are there for them. However, don't interfere unless they ask for assistance. They will request your help if it is needed. Take your business elsewhere if your current bank or financial institution is letting services slip or is not supportive. Remember, they need customers just as you need their services.

Tuesday the 21st. As an Aries, you welcome any opportunity to see the world or broaden your outlook. Wonderful travel plans may involve visiting loved ones and relatives overseas. The chance to mix with people from different backgrounds and to sample diverse customs appeals to the adventurous. Even news of a possible mix-up with travel documents won't do much to dampen your spirits.

Wednesday the 22nd. An opportunity to further your education through a seminar or training course arises. Even if the subject is not that appealing, take up the offer. It could prove to be an enlightening experience. Ask your spiritual friends to recommend a good reader and have your palm read for extra insight. Indulge in activities you love at the end of a long and busy day.

Thursday the 23rd. Today contains both a promise and a warning. The Sun enters Virgo, emphasizing health, work, and daily life. Employment situations are likely to improve for the better. Problems that have plagued you should be finally resolved. Overestimating your capabilities could result in not taking enough care with general health and well-being. Take frequent rest breaks and drink plenty of fluids.

Friday the 24th. Your everyday routine could be disrupted by coworkers or your employer. A boss is likely to saddle you with responsibilities belonging to others. Don't grumble. With efficiency and organizational skills to spare, extra tasks are easily handled. A pioneering spirit also blends easily with your mental and physical energies. A new business venture begun now should turn out to be lucrative.

Saturday the 25th. The hustle and bustle of city life is something you could do without. Pack your bags and find somewhere quiet for an indulgent retreat. Read a book under a shady tree, meditate, or stroll around in open spaces. Steer clear of those who require all your time and attention. You will be more likely to be pushy or impatient with others. Do what you need to do by yourself.

Sunday the 26th. You are in a much better frame of mind today. So unless you lose sight of your goals, everything should be working in your favor. Positive connections can be made. You will appreciate the company of friends, family, and people who are on the same wavelength as you. Pleasure comes from sharing points of view and philosophies. An idea could pay off in a big way if developed sufficiently.

Weekly Summary

Romance is still in the air, with invitations to engagements or weddings likely. Plans for your own wedding or special celebration may be accelerating as the guest list continues to grow. If you are on a strict budget and you exceed it, be ruthless. Trim the list and limit invitations to family and special friends. Pleasing results from an investment could bring monetary gains.

The Sun and Mercury, the planet of thinking processes, are now visiting Virgo in your house of health, work, and service. Attention to detail is enhanced, as you are looking for perfection. Singles might be attracted to an older or more mature partner. Take more interest in health. Focus on your nutritional needs and overall well-being.

You could be in a situation that calls for innovation, which can test your resolve. But you should enjoy the chance to do battle. Don't allow coworkers to convince you to do or take part in something that you don't believe in or feel is not appropriate. Distance yourself from any troublemakers. Charisma is strong, but make sure this doesn't lead to cheating on a partner.

35th Week/August 27–September 2

Monday the 27th. The lack of objectivity from a superior is likely to cause irritation. Hang in there. Eventually others will realize the error of their ways. Vindication will come. Just be patient. Change your plans if socializing with friends is not on the agenda tonight. Arrange an impromptu meal at a favorite restaurant, ring family to arrange a visit, or drop into usual haunts where friends hang out.

Tuesday the 28th. Today's eclipsed Full Moon in Pisces ensures that keeping boredom at bay won't be a problem. On the other hand, slowing down and paying attention to details will be. Acting on impulse will likely land you in hot water. Avoid rash behavior. If health issues arise, this could be another reason to stop rushing around. Listen to your body. It may be trying to tell you something important.

Wednesday the 29th. Decisions concerning studies that will enhance your qualifications or career prospects may prove difficult. Trust your instincts and wait a few days before making concrete plans. That way you can make different arrangements should you have second thoughts. Compassion and sensitivity are heightened. Joining a charitable group brings its own rewards.

Thursday the 30th. Work off nervous energy by keeping busy. Work in the garden or make time for those household chores you haven't had time to finish. Think how happy you will feel when outstanding tasks are completed. A partner may need your assistance. Make sure to provide moral support. You would expect similar treatment if placed in the same situation.

Friday the 31st. Don't be afraid to stand out from others. Taking small risks can pay dividends. Devote special attention to a personal project. Extra care with your diet may be necessary. A minor illness or allergy could be triggered by consuming something you are allergic to. Cultural events can prove to be enlightening experiences for the whole family.

Saturday September 1st Rise slowly and enjoy a leisurely breakfast before the day's activities. Over the next week, proceed with caution. Impatient Mars challenges disruptive Uranus, bringing turmoil for the foolhardy. Reckless action is likely to cause an incident, as you are inclined toward impulsiveness now. Seek amusement that keeps you moving but does not pose a risk to personal safety.

Sunday the 2nd. Applying discipline could be a challenge for the easygoing Ram. Although practical action might seem undesirable, it may be necessary. You could go overboard in most activities you pursue now. Curb impulses to spend rashly. If you feel tense or anxious, engage in light exercise, play a sport, or go dancing to keep the energy flowing.

Weekly Summary

Friends and relatives may seek your help and guidance. Don't take sides if this involves more than one person. Communications with those from other countries or cultures can be interesting and informative. Record the information you get, as this can assist your career or business progress. Care should be taken that you don't overestimate either your capabilities or the time available to meet current commitments.

Dreams and fantasies are in focus. Imagination and inspiration are strengthened. Talented Aries can do work that requires a creative touch and artistic flair. The lunar eclipse during the Full Moon in Pisces helps you finish projects. Be on guard, though, as you could be easily swayed by emotions. Someone may take advantage of your current sensitive mood, especially if you feel guilty about something.

Procrastination could cause problems. Take care of tasks or issues that have been left unfinished. You cannot afford to let them linger any longer. Guard what you say, as you have a tendency to be blunt and tactless. Practice the art of diplomacy, and relationships should remain harmonious. A small gamble could pay off if you apply common sense.

36th Week/September 3–9

Monday the 3rd. Saturn, planet of discipline, will reside in Virgo in your health sector for the next couple of years and will encourage a healthier lifestyle. Remember the saying that what goes through the lips ends up on the hips. Drink plenty of filtered water and reduce your intake of fattening foods. Consistent exercise can soon bring the body back into shape. Routine work and duties will be more enjoyable, not as boring as usual.

Tuesday the 4th. Quell any urges to stick your nose into other people's business. Advice given can be beneficial as long as it is asked for. Think about the ripples that may result if you overstep the mark. Stay true to your word in matters of the heart and reap the rewards. Special time spent with your lover brings joy and the feeling of being more in love than ever.

Wednesday the 5th. You are in the mood to nurture your nearest and dearest. Gather friends and loved ones around for a delicious home-cooked meal. Add your own creative stroke of magic to provide a special touch. Communicative Mercury now enters Libra in your sector of relationships and will accentuate teamwork. Cooperation is important both on the job and with your loved ones.

Thursday the 6th. Don't overreact if things go wrong today. Most situations will work out better than you expect. Making your home a haven appeals to Aries. You may need space on an emotional and physical level. Remove old objects that have outlived their usefulness. Avoid decision making, especially in the early evening. Instead, soak in a warm tub and relax.

Friday the 7th. Pace yourself today. A demanding issue could be taking its toll. Stop pushing yourself and take time out to restore your vital inner energies. Education features strongly as powerhouse Pluto has moved in direct motion in your Sagittarius sector of higher learning. Opportunities to advance your knowledge or enter a new training course exist now.

Saturday the 8th. Graceful Venus now moves forward in Leo in your sector of self-expression. Creative pastimes left dormant could become of interest again. Friends might insist that you join in social activities even though arrangements may not appeal. Compromise by attending and then leave early. Reach out to family and friends. Mend fences and build new bridges.

Sunday the 9th. Abundant energy is likely today. But be careful how you handle it. You may be tempted to push yourself harder than usual. Aries looking for a better paying job could spend time updating resumes and scouring the employment ads. Enjoy lighthearted discussions with friends. Gossip about the latest movies, magazines, or who among you are single or currently part of a couple.

Weekly Summary

The new week heralds a major planetary shift. Heavyweight Saturn has entered Virgo for a two-year transit. The focus now shifts to conditions surrounding your daily routine, health, and employment. Becoming firmer, fitter, and healthier and losing weight should be easier, as long as a regular exercise and diet program are in place and maintained.

High energy combined with a restless mood indicates that concentration may be difficult to maintain. Staying focused hinges on keeping distractions out of reach. Remove magazines and books from view, switch off the TV, and keep your office or front door closed. Vary your daily routine as much as possible, and add interest by taking a different route to work.

Consider the pros and cons before making or agreeing to firm commitments. You can be inclined to speak and act first before you think about possible later consequences. This also applies to spending habits. Creative projects started now should have a fresh appeal with Venus now direct. Romance could blossom with someone you meet through a casual contact.

37th Week/September 10–16

Monday the 10th. Don't be surprised if opposition to work ideas or projects is encountered. Be wary of those who offer challenges and then attempt to take credit for your efforts when things proceed better than expected. Make sure your health and physical fitness are in good form by addressing any ailments or illness. Arrange appointments with your health-care adviser if problems persist.

Tuesday the 11th. Put your best foot forward and be ready to perform on the job. An authority figure may be impressed by your discipline and sense of responsibility. Brace yourself for changes at work. Even if you feel you are not ready for new arrangements, give it a trial. The eclipsed Virgo New Moon paves the way for improved employment conditions and procedures.

Wednesday the 12th. A secret might be revealed. Being the last to know may be upsetting. Find out why you were left out of the loop before making wild accusations. There may be an obvious reason why, but you just cannot see it. If problems exist in your intimate relationship, open up and seek answers. Discuss issues with your partner. You can both handle current problems.

Thursday the 13th. Aries usually relishes being on the move, and that is what you may be doing for most of the day. If you have been committing too much of your time and energy to voluntary efforts, take a step back. Let others pitch in and do their share. You can then spend more time with loved ones or participate in pursuits of your choice. Socialize with those you see on a regular basis tonight.

Friday the 14th. Take it easy this morning. Relax and don't rush if you are not expected anywhere. Future security and financial worth dominate your thinking. Put in place strategies to grow your nest egg. Positive results are likely. However, delay discussions for a few days if you share resources with another. If who pays for what is a sore point, wait until the mood feels right before going ahead.

Saturday the 15th. Imagination and inspiration are strengthened. Wishes could come true, so be careful what you wish for. Ensure that joint monetary affairs are in order. Confirm that insurance payments have been made and accounts that affect financial security are up to date. Emotions and sexual feelings are stimulated, enabling you to work on your intimate relationship to keep it stable and viable.

Sunday the 16th. Try to catch a few extra winks this morning to remain in top form. Endeavor to be more patient and forgiving, and beware issuing ultimatums around the home. Your words are likely to fall on deaf ears, or you could get more back than you bargained for. Take a friend's suggestion to do something entirely different from your usual routine. Choose recreational pursuits that bring pleasure and variety.

Weekly Summary

Pace yourself. Energy levels remain high, causing you to take on too many commitments or push yourself too hard. Continue to monitor spending. Impulsive and extravagant urges can wreck the household budget if care is not applied. Gains can be made by working in conjunction with coworkers or business associates rather than going solo.

A solar eclipse during New Moon in Virgo encourages you to talk about whatever is uppermost in your mind. If you are not happy with current employment conditions, arrange a meeting with a boss to discuss the changes you want. Apply the same principles if your health is causing concern. Make an appointment to see your health-care practitioner.

The prospects for job seekers finding suitable work increases. Domestic and home-based activities will demand more time and attention. Do a big cleanup around the house and garden over the next two weeks. Make sure those you live with pull their weight.

38th Week/September 17–23

Monday the 17th. Bask in a mate's affection. Sharing interests with each other can help your relationship to evolve. Take care that discussions don't involve politics or religion. Otherwise, disharmony could spoil a congenial atmosphere. Some tasks on today's agenda could easily be done by other people. Let go and let others take the lead.

Tuesday the 18th. Your ability to bring inspiring dialogue to those around you is enhanced. Whatever message you convey should be easily understood. Sales presentations, talks, or general discussions are likely to be persuasive and informative. This is a favorable time to purchase something of value for your home or garden, providing you don't spend more than the bank balance can afford.

Wednesday the 19th. The atmosphere surrounding Rams could be a little tense. Aries considering an adventurous vacation should reexamine your finances before confirming travel dates. Underestimating expenses could be dangerous. Do the figures again to make sure. It is better to have too much than not enough. Reduce the pressure in your life by scheduling less on your social and personal calendar. Progress can still be made.

Thursday the 20th. Disagreeable or frustrating chores are easily managed and will yield positive results. Family matters also take on importance. Rearrange your time to include more hours with loved ones and less on the job. Making overseas travel plans should be a relaxed and happy experience, with anticipation mounting. Concentration is abundant, and you are likely to be very serious about your work.

Friday the 21st. Embrace diplomacy and make discretion your new catchword. Contracts in process might finally reach a resolution. With your ruler Mars opposing the powerful Pluto, domestic and workplace spats could quickly sour any situation. Confusion around a love affair or being let down by a lover is likely to bring disappointment. Try to remain objective and don't view any situations as a personal failure.

Saturday the 22nd. You could feel that others rolled out of the wrong side of bed this morning. Calm reasoning is the best way to handle the mental agitation of others. As an Aries you are not usually a team player. You prefer to go it alone. However, group settings can be fun and friendly if you give it a try. A new contract could mean you are asked to work longer hours. Jump at this chance to earn extra money.

Sunday the 23rd. The Sun now visits your opposite sign of Libra until October 23. Attention is drawn toward those close to you in a personal or professional relationship. Social participation and group interaction can open doors. Positive outcomes are likely if you apply effort and pursue contacts made. This can be an opportune period for public-relation activities, legal contests, and team pursuits.

Weekly Summary

Spending time with like-minded people or those who share similar interests appeals to Aries looking for companionship. Practical matters may be disregarded for more relaxing and spiritual activities. Leave the humdrum world of reality for a little while and escape into fantasy land. Listen to music, read romance novels, or paint flowers or sea scenes to soothe the soul.

Thoughts of love as well as pleasure take priority. Singles should look closer to home for romantic interludes. Close relationships thrive, with couples sharing happy rapport throughout the week. Creative urges and imagination are stimulated, increasing artistic expression of your natural talents. Recognition for work produced is likely. Extra cash could be generated through hobbies or recreational pursuits.

Words roll off your tongue easily, and your lectures are likely to be applauded by an appreciative audience. Expect a heavier than usual workload, which could require overtime to keep on top of your responsibilities. With the Sun visiting Libra in your sector of professional and permanent partnerships, romantic prospects increase, and you may be in popular demand socially.

39th Week/September 24–30

Monday the 24th. Logic and reality are essential in making decisions. Add Aries optimism and courage, and you can realize goals much sooner. Others find inspiration in your behavior and what you have to say. Original schemes and ideas can take concrete form. You could be involved in a political discussion in which you can excel. However, take care that tact and diplomacy are on display.

Tuesday the 25th. Spend time visualizing exactly how you would like your future to be, and you will aid your progress. Success is more likely if ambitions are kept in sight. Try something with a mystical or spiritual theme for amusement. A good chance exists that this could appeal and become a passion. Put yourself and your needs first tonight. Stay home and let others socialize without you.

Wednesday the 26th. Choose your company carefully. Patience will be limited with those you consider dull or sticklers for routine. If your usual attire is casual, it won't hurt to dress up a little more. You never know who is around the corner to impress and to further your cause. Today's Aries Full Moon indicates sensitive feelings and possible problems with the key people in your life.

Thursday the 27th. Mercury is now in attendance in Scorpio, bringing attention to monies and assets you share with others. Any issues in this area should be sorted out to ensure continued financial security and stability. Try a session with a recommended financial adviser to ease current money pressures. It cannot do any harm and may prove to be so beneficial you wonder why you persisted so long without assistance.

Friday the 28th. Distractions are the likely cause of numerous mistakes now. Leave complex tasks and problems until next week when you can start afresh. Shocks and surprises are in store for Aries with large share holdings. It is not the time to commit any more funds, especially if it involves joint finances. Implement gentle stress-relief measures this evening to relax.

Saturday the 29th. Domestic affairs and family matters are strongly influenced by energetic Mars, now residing in Cancer. Home-improvement plans or a busy agenda of entertaining centers around your domestic quarters. Utilize creative skills to enhance your environment and to organize special celebrations. Ambitious ideas and plans put into action move closer to reality now.

Sunday the 30th. Lots of activity and movement is promised today. Sudden insights, new discoveries, and the ability to come up with fresh solutions to pressing issues ensure a productive and busy time ahead. An inheritance or windfall might be received, or an invest-ment can finally pay dividends. A significant conversa-tion or some good news adds zest to the day. Go visiting, play a sport, see a movie. Just don't stay in.

Weekly Summary

Plenty of action and variety are on your plate. A patient attitude is rarely seen in Aries and may be missing again. Tolerance needs to be cultivated if you want to remain in the good graces of family, friends, and coworkers. Tread warily, as the Full Moon in your sign of Aries heats up emotions.

Focus on personal grooming and appearance. You have an eye for style and flair. Treat yourself to a massage or an expensive beauty lotion. Update your wardrobe, make changes to your hair color, purchase trendy cos-tume jewelry to complement or complete the new you. Looking and feeling good on the outside brings inner confidence.

Joint financial responsibilities and investments pros-per during Mercury's visit in Scorpio. But domestic tranquillity may be in short supply from now until the end of the year because your ruler Mars is in Cancer in your house of home and family. Ongoing projects affecting living conditions can be more challenging and problematical than expected.

40th Week/October 1–7

Monday October 1st. It is not unusual for Aries to be on the move, always running from one place to another. Today this might seem like it is never ending. You may not be overly enthralled by some of the jobs on your to-do list either. Unexpected attention from a romantic possibility could be a pleasant surprise. If love falls into your personal space, lap it up and enjoy the moment.

Tuesday the 2nd. An entertaining and possibly fiery day awaits, and that is just during working hours. Don't be hung up or overwhelmed with everyday life or household chores that await you. Enjoy the here and now and do what you can. Make a list and cross off items as you deal with them to avoid forgetting anything that may be urgent or important. Last-minute social arrangements should provide relaxation.

Wednesday the 3rd. A great deal of passion exists around interactions with others. Luck comes by getting out and mingling with others. What may have begun as a lighthearted romance could suddenly change for the better. If you have been hoping for a romantic getaway, this is the day to begin your journey or at least plan an interlude for a future time.

Thursday the 4th. Don't allow antagonism with a family member to develop into open warfare. Ignoring the emotional outbursts of others could ease the tension. Be prepared to reschedule a lunch date or make changes to romantic arrangements. You may have more than your usual social activities to attend over the coming weeks, prompting a need to keep your diary up to date.

Friday the 5th. Many Rams may have something to celebrate. There is an increased possibility of receiving a wedding invitation, a proposal, or you could hear news of a family member's engagement. A magnetic effect attracts others to you. Making new alliances could come in handy later on if you take time to cultivate contacts. Harmony at home should prevail, with sweet romance abundant for Aries lovers.

Saturday the 6th. A productive day looms for creativity and injecting new ideas into work-related projects. Keep alert. The ability to recognize fresh opportunities assists Aries intent on quickly moving up the career ladder. Stay cool if you have the opportunity to meet a celebrity or someone you admire. Your calm and relaxed manner could make an indelible impression.

Sunday the 7th. You are in the mood to expand your horizons on a local scale. An impromptu trip into the countryside can delight the youngsters and should prove to be an enjoyable day for the whole family. Rather than pay for expensive meals, add to the fun and pack a picnic lunch. If it is too cold to eat outdoors, be daring. Find a sheltered spot and huddle with your favorite companion.

Weekly Summary

In true Aries fashion you rush around trying to get everything done at once. Your schedule could include many things you have or have not done before as well as those that are not usually your responsibility. Make extra concessions and create more harmony around the home. If you do need to issue demands, exercise tact to receive the support you need.

Relationships with women can be improved if effort is applied. If you are a parent of older children, don't smother them. Allow youngsters more independence so they can spread their wings and gain confidence. A chance to meet an important person or celebrity could see your photo in the news or on TV, possibly bringing five minutes of fame. Expect to hear some exciting news.

Your creative drive and your sexual drive and your motivation are on fire. If you are single the desire to find a passionate and loving partner intensifies. Aries are known for boldness, so you could even make the first move with happy results. A healthier bank balance could come through a hobby that becomes a new source of income. Special celebrations bring joy.

41st Week/October 8–14

Monday the 8th. Personal relationships are important to emotional health and well-being, and today brings the trends you need. Projects around the house that have been waiting for action can commence now. Creative Venus is now visiting Virgo, the sign of order and service. Get out the decorating magazines and plan changes to brighten up your house, apartment, or trailer.

Tuesday the 9th. Subtly publicize your creative and artistic talents, especially to those with whom you work. You could receive an irresistible offer if you do. Attend to neglected health matters. It may be just that you need to rest more to restore vitality. If you feel confused about an emotional issue, be assured that it is not as complex as you think. Perhaps you are not seeing things as clearly as you usually do.

Wednesday the 10th. Mercury, planet of information, will move retrograde on Friday, heralding a period when communication goes haywire, travel arrangements are disrupted, and computers are more likely to crash or become infected with a virus. Start to think through and reconsider previous ideas, especially those relating to debts, loans, or taxes.

Thursday the 11th. The Libra New Moon urges you to finalize legal contracts and deeds. Concentrate on the fine print. Minor details missed could become major issues later on. A public presentation should be well received. You may contact important people who could provide guidance in steering you toward cherished aims. Expect a bundle of romance and affection from your special love.

Friday the 12th. Now is a good time to look ahead. Review a vacation plan, plot a career move, or reexamine where your relationship is heading. While you are reorganizing your affairs, don't forget to allocate funds for your bills. Also, revise the household budget and assign some funds for your savings plan. Spending money to impress others may be costly. Make sure that purchases are really what you need and not frivolous.

Saturday the 13th. Take the opportunity to create your own happiness. The potential exists to fall in love with an older coworker. If affectionate bonds are returned, don't worry about the age difference. Love can conquer all. A tighter hold on the purse strings may be essential. Poring over bills and accounts may not be much fun if this is your day off but is necessary to retain peace of mind.

Sunday the 14th. Whether you take a short trip, slip away for a quiet interlude, or do something different, you will enjoy an escape from the mundane tasks of everyday life. Planning an overseas trip with a friend might appeal to active Aries. Although your arrangements may be mainly pleasure based, add destinations you are anxious to learn more about to expand your knowledge.

Weekly Summary

Most Aries thrive on activity and adventure. Plans for an upcoming trip may be your focus now. Organizing time off, finalizing work commitments, and training others on the job keep you busy but could also take a toll on health and energy. Expect wonderful things to occur in the domestic scene. Your honesty and integrity will be appreciated.

Success could be enjoyed through public relations, investments, or a small windfall that can help pay the bills. Expect some indecision on your part once Mercury goes into retrograde motion Friday. Complications could also emerge concerning communication mix-ups, traffic delays, and mechanical failures. Make time to relax with loved ones, family, or your loving partner.

At week's end making plans should be easier, but sticking with daily routine proves challenging. Interruptions, distractions, and restlessness can delay work progress. Sorting out joint finances won't be a problem if you follow the guidance of a friend who is a whiz with money. Cleaning, decorating, and completing household chores may be a labor of love.

42nd Week/October 15–21

Monday the 15th. A more relaxed day provides the chance to catch up on neglected personal activities. You are in the mood to focus on things of prime importance to you and are content to allow the rest of the world to do the same. Creative urges prompt a trip to the theater or movies. Romance is also likely this evening as couples share happy rapport and singles look for love.

Tuesday the 16th. This can be an exciting day. The potential to increase your moneymaking ability could come through an offer of a new job or partnership venture. Providing you are prepared for minor hiccups and delays, prospects are bright. Good news may concern a partner's ability to generate extra income through promotion, salary increase, or a larger than usual commission check.

Wednesday the 17th. The cosmos is sending good vibes for a number of things, including romance. It is also a starred time to marry, propose, or to be proposed to. A boost to morale and status comes from being in the spotlight. Efforts to promote your ambitions should prove rewarding. Appointments, meetings, or interviews with business or financial people are likely to have positive outcomes.

Thursday the 18th. Your excellent track record could mean that additional responsibilities will be heaped on you. If coping with extra duties means less time spent with loved ones, speak up now before it is too late. Accept any invitation to raise your public profile and increase your experience of appearing before others. Bear in mind that moves made now are also likely to bring future financial benefits.

Friday the 19th. Cultivating old friendships are just as important as making new ones. Put this in perspective and refrain from idealizing newcomers who join your friendship circle. You may want to escape work today, even though you know it won't happen because others are relying on your guidance. Give yourself a break. Arrange to start earlier than usual and leave by lunchtime.

Saturday the 20th. Life should take on a rosier glow today. There is a buzz around socializing with friends and colleagues now. Home alone is not where you are meant to be. Arrange to visit or meet companions for coffee. Take action to restore a friendship or association that has been the cause of angst. A positive overture made now should work wonders.

Sunday the 21st. Take a trip to special childhood haunts. Sights and sounds recall beautiful memories of things long past. Seeing for yourself just how far you have traveled along life's path can open your eyes for future progress. You may be worried about a partner's unsaid words. Use compassion to draw them out and you can give guidance and understanding.

Weekly Summary

Whether your schedule includes work, travel, study to broaden your knowledge, or researching for a set goal, make plans early. Create deadlines to steadily work toward so you remain on track and make progress. If you are organized, achievements are easier and can come more quickly than you thought possible. Make sure you complete what you start before moving on.

Attending a conference could put you in touch with like-minded people. You may even make one or several new best friends to share your interests or concerns. For singles, this could also lead to the start of a beautiful romance. Your financial outlook looks more stable, as chances to generate income through professional advancement are on the increase.

Someone has to take center stage, so why not jump in and enhance your reputation as well as raise your profile? Let others see what you are capable of, especially those in a position of power. Listening to words of wisdom from a colleague who has your best interests at heart could help shorten your journey to the top.

43rd Week/October 22–28

Monday the 22nd. A sick or lonely friend can benefit from your compassion and generosity. Visiting others in a hospital or at a home offers unexpected rewards for all to share. Distinguishing between fact and fantasy could be difficult right now, as there may be a lot going on in your head. Work behind the scenes or where distractions are minimal to keep on top, and avoid making important decisions today.

Tuesday the 23rd. Now the Sun is visiting Scorpio until November 22, promising opportunities for change and the chance to invest in your future progress. Emotional contacts with loved ones are likely to be more intense throughout this period. Apply caution. Endeavoring to exert power over others or coercing them into doing things they are not happy about can cause resentment.

Wednesday the 24th. Tension and stress form part of the day. Therapy helps Aries with money and time to spare. Gardening or visiting customers for a social chat can be of assistance in easing your anxiety and reducing stress. Pay extra attention to everything that you and others say to avoid slipups or misunderstandings. Say exactly what you mean and nothing more. Be more assertive when it comes to your priorities.

Thursday the 25th. You may be inclined to take more risks than usual. A business or financial investment may pay dividends. Nevertheless, caution needs to be applied, as at times you are inclined to impulsive or reckless behavior. A personal decision regarding a joint money matter could bring opposition from a partner. Seek a compromise that both of you can live with.

Friday the 26th. A prickly issue is likely to get under your skin. This is almost certain to involve problems with money, as the Taurus Full Moon is highlighting your personal financial sector now. You will look at your bank balance and wonder where all the money has gone. Be warned. If you try to bring this up with your partner, expect an argument before a resolution is found.

Saturday the 27th. Attend to minor financial details. An inclination for the good things of life means you don't need a lot of encouragement to splurge. Your time would be better spent pondering various options on ways to cut costs in the household budget and improve your financial state. Emotions may play tricks, so be careful not to commit to anything that makes you uncomfortable.

Sunday the 28th. Friends might try to talk you into something you don't want to do. Remain firm. Giving in could encourage their behavior to continue and place you in a tricky situation. It may be time to test the friendship and explain your reasons for saying no. Short trips may be tiring but enjoyable. If driving, take care on the roads and avoid weekend traffic delays by leaving for destinations early.

Weekly Summary

On Tuesday the Sun enters Scorpio and your eighth house, encouraging you to become more in tune with your inner feelings. This is the time to let go of past clutter and move ahead with clarity. Allow for change to take place without fearing that control is being handed over to others. Having faith and believing in self is good for confidence as long as you also include a healthy dose of humility.

On Wednesday a retrograde Mercury backtracks into Libra in your house of professional and personal partnerships. This influence can help you to understand a partner's reactions on a deeper level. Once you are able to comprehend past issues, you will know what needs to be avoided in the future.

Even if your inclination is to gloss over details, time can be saved if you slow down and become more methodical. Avoid hidden matters that involve a relative or neighbor. Don't take things at face value. Something strange may be afoot. You could be tempted to over-spend on something you really want but don't need. Give it some thought before making a final decision.

44th Week/October 29–November 4

Monday the 29th. Clear thinking is important because attempts at resolving family issues may be tricky. The potential to stir the pot even more is possible if you take an aggressive or impatient stance. Expressing yourself quietly and clearly would have a better chance of any disagreement being resolved. Singles might begin to view a colleague through eyes of passion. Stay cool and detached. The object of your desires may not have the same feelings.

Tuesday the 30th. Whether you are buying, selling, moving, or renovating, there is bound to be action around family and property. A cherished objective could become reality for you. Stress and pressure may get the better of you as patience with family members begins to wane. Hop on the exercise bike, do sit-ups, or run around the block to renew energy and regain composure.

Wednesday the 31st. Misunderstandings and confusing influences surround the morning. Verify facts before giving information that may be false or grossly exaggerated. It is a favorable time for any Aries currently working from home. Plan your schedule, screen calls, and you may be surprised at the amount of work you zip through. Entertainment plans that involve family groups might be disrupted.

Thursday November 1st. Mercury, planet of movement, goes direct in Libra today. Take an assertive approach to your financial investments. If you are not receiving results for your time, effort, and energy, look for other areas for increased dividends. Creative problem solving on the job raises your worth. Inform others of your ideas and solutions.

Friday the 2nd. Put off tasks that require clear thinking this morning. Don't disappoint yourself or others. There is a chance that you won't work up to your usual high standard. Watch for the tendency to spend too much on entertainment. If you have a big weekend ahead, it may be better for the wallet and your health to try for an early night. Your ruler Mars connects with the Moon around midnight, interrupting slumber and making it difficult to return to sleep.

Saturday the 3rd. Take an interest in fitness, diet, and other health matters. If you must drink, do it in moderation, especially at social events with people you want to impress. Instead of your hard work finally showing results, over-indulgence could derail efforts to improve your lifestyle. Influential people may be impressed with your wisdom, flow of ideas, and articulate manner of expression. They will keep noticing if you retain your composure.

Sunday the 4th. Aries are charged with more than usual high energy today. However, the temptation to over-indulge remains. Keeping cravings under control tests your resolve if you have a sweet tooth. Since you are not in the mood to play the nice guy, choose your company carefully. You could be sorry if patience wears thin and you enter into a verbal clash with those who push your buttons.

Weekly Summary

Lots of outside influences pulling you this way and that way may make it difficult to get a handle on what needs to be done. Friends or family could contribute to many of your irritations with words spoken either in jest or anger. Think about advice you receive. It may not appear to be helpful now but could be in the future.

As an energetic Aries you often pay little attention to health and physical needs. But your willpower is at low ebb, which isn't good news if you are on a strict health regimen or a diet. Good intentions are likely to vanish at the first hint of temptation. Try to put space between you and your favorite fattening food. If you do indulge, work off calories with exercise or go for a vigorous hike.

Mercury moving forward again brings an end to confusion around a partnership issue without any conscious effort on your part. Expressing creative ideas or a special talent should prove successful. Spending habits could be still under a cloud. You may be irresistibly attracted to the luxurious and expensive, causing issues with a partner or loved ones. Compromise will be the key to maintaining a balance.

45th Week/November 5–11

Monday the 5th. A delayed work project or one you have been patiently waiting for could finally arrive. Savor the moment. You deserve it. Visiting a new mother could be a joyous occasion and the reason to bring out the champagne and celebrate the birth in style. A social outing with business overtones could raise your partner's profile.

Tuesday the 6th. Emotions could take control of your life, bringing heated clashes with a partner or loved one. Being overly melodramatic can exaggerate the situation, and tempers might flare. Either you or a family member could also make a big fuss over money, turning it into something larger than it actually is. Try not to overreact. Encourage others to follow your cool, calm example.

Wednesday the 7th. Exciting vibes surround Aries, with love and passion still in focus. Singles should choose a lover carefully or suffer later regret. You are in top form with the motivation and desire to succeed. This can inspire you to make the most of any potential that comes along. Leadership qualities are enhanced. With your current optimism, anything is possible. Push the limits now in order to get the maximum effect.

Thursday the 8th. Venus, goddess of luck and love, enters Libra in your relationship zone, bringing special magic to share with professional and intimate partners. Opportunities resulting in higher earnings may be presented. Stay alert. If you are owed money and all efforts to collect have failed, now is the time to initiate proceedings. Offer one last chance to pay up before you take legal action.

Friday the 9th. Make the most of today's celestial energies. A New Moon in Scorpio can have a beneficial influence on partnership funds, business profits, and resources. Gains could come by paying closer attention to your future security needs. If the door of opportunity is stuck, now is the time to push it open. You could produce an unexpected outcome that provides the advantage you were seeking.

Saturday the 10th. If you have issues that need addressing, be honest and go straight to the point. Lay your cards on the table. Skirting around the truth to make yourself or others feel better is a recipe for disaster. Someone might consider your views on a particular subject excessive, but you are unlikely to soften your stance. Try to be less extreme. Socializing with those you know well boosts self-esteem this evening.

Sunday the 11th. Although you have your fair share of friends, finding out that one of them has let you down is upsetting. If your patience is exhausted by constantly dealing with the problems of close companions, perhaps it's time to look objectively at your friendship circle. Cull those who are no longer loyal. Don't make the day all about effort. Get the brain firing with study, puzzles, or video games.

Weekly Summary

Domestic issues are likely to bring disagreements that cause stress. Agree to disagree if issues look like they could get out of hand with a partner, parent, or roommate. If you are upset about relationship problems, immerse yourself in something that makes you forget for a little while. Clean, cook, go for a walk, work out at the gym, or perhaps shop to help ease the blues.

Venus, the planet that rules personal magnetism, will be visiting Libra in your professional and personal partnership sector. Venus here helps to improve relationships and negotiate an important agreement. A business partnership could come under scrutiny. Be very careful about who and what you promote, and resist any temptation to indulge in get-rich-quick schemes.

The Scorpio New Moon encourages you to extend the range of your business activities and to place more importance on funds shared with others. Future security comes from a positive and expansive attitude. Experience should show that the more effort you put into achieving goals, the higher the chance of success. Collect any outstanding debts to ensure your finances remain solid.

46th Week/November 12–18

Monday the 12th. Someone may be trying to trip you up. There might not be much you can do, but don't give further ammunition. If a newcomer suddenly takes your fancy and appears absolutely captivating, proceed with caution. You probably know in your heart of hearts that this is not a good situation. But you could persuade yourself how truly wonderful everything is. Enjoy the feeling but avoid getting trapped.

Tuesday the 13th. Hard work and selfless duty can provide the acknowledgment you crave and deserve. Look around you and find something you no longer need. It could be a thoughtful gift for a friend or deserving person. An involvement in team situations may not be easy, especially if some members are not working in unison. Take the lead and find a middle road where others can express themselves but still move ahead in the same direction.

Wednesday the 14th. Apply diplomacy plus if you need cooperation. Overassertiveness could be met with anger, and you might end up not knowing how to finish what you began. Something exciting could emerge concerning ideas, business, or creative projects. Demands on your time may be heavy, so consider reducing your workload. Becoming overly involved in your work may cause a rift with a lover.

Thursday the 15th. Your ruler, dynamo Mars, moves into retrograde mode until the end of January 2008. This presents Aries with an opportunity to concentrate energy into completing difficult tasks and projects, particularly those relating to the domestic scene. A competitive spirit prevails. Use the impetus to succeed in areas that might seem impossible to conquer.

Friday the 16th. As a fire sign you tend to thrive on new challenges. It piques a desire to show off your capabilities. Commitment to your future is strong, and you know what you want. Decisions made now could change the course of your life. But be sure you know what you are letting yourself in for before venturing too far along the track. Friends may be able to provide a helping hand. Don't be too proud to let others help you.

Saturday the 17th. If you have been resisting the idea of organizing your next vacation, you might decide that you cannot wait any longer. Destinations that include an overseas journey could bring the stimulation you seek. Acting erratically in relationships might be the cause of problems. A sudden infatuation, or an impulse to be free, or the desire to make radical changes in a current relationship needs to be handled with care.

Sunday the 18th. If you are shopping, you may be intrigued by things that boost self-confidence or can help in furthering your goals and aspirations. You could find just the right outfit for a job interview or important meeting. Problems with loved ones could arise. Take care that you are not given a family project that may be more than you can handle. Put your own responsibilities first.

Weekly Summary

Inadequacies and flaws in those you consider your friends may be particularly worrisome. If the attitudes and behavior of others no longer fit in with your values, it may be time to part company and develop new friendships. You may feel overwhelmed if you try to complete all chores and duties by yourself. Make it easier on yourself. Delegate or ask for assistance.

An all-or-nothing attitude is likely to urge you to be more proactive. If there is something you always wanted to teach or demonstrate, now is a good time to start. Locate a place, advertise your starting date, and let interested parties know of your intention. Business owners should be certain before splurging on a special event to increase sales.

Your ruler Mars turns retrograde in Cancer in your sector of home and family affairs. This is a good time to put extra effort into household projects, repairs, and renovations. Your ability to stay focused on tasks that require a long and arduous input is enhanced, resulting in many accomplishments from now through January 2008. Ongoing family arguments can be resolved to everyone's satisfaction if the effort is made to bring peace to warring parties.

47th Week/November 19–25

Monday the 19th. Communication is a strong point today, which could lead to a fiery discussion with loved ones over matters close to home. You can persuade others to see things your way providing you don't become huffy and bad tempered. Formulate plans to install or upgrade your home security as an extra precaution against unwanted intruders. Lock up securely if you are not staying in today.

Tuesday the 20th. Try not to focus on trivial matters. Irritation could quickly surface, especially if you are around quarrelsome people. Personal doubts and insecurities could be a preoccupation, making decisions difficult. Banish these and replace them with faith and positive thoughts. Avoid financial involvements with others, in particular with a friend who has a habit of not repaying loans.

Wednesday the 21st. Avoid accidents around the home by maintaining sensible precautions. Walk, don't run, and remove obstacles hazardous to your personal safety. You might be feeling especially needed as your partner requests your support with a special function. Sudden bright ideas could really pay off. Write these down and start researching the possibilities.

Thursday the 22nd. The Sun now moves into fiery Sagittarius, sign of independence, tempting many Aries to get up and go. Current adventurous influences urge you to explore and to try many different things. The prospect of travel conveys excitement. Scholastic interests come to the fore, providing motivation to examine ways to further your education, training, and knowledge.

Friday the 23rd. Steer clear of important investment matters today. There is a danger of being totally misled if you don't retain a sense of reality. If you haven't made a considerable dent in your festive shopping, it would be a prudent idea to work out a strict budget before you head for the stores. Taking only the cash you can afford to spend is another way to avoid parting with more than you should.

Saturday the 24th. Today's Gemini Full Moon advises Aries to keep your nose out of others' affairs. To avoid a confrontation, be mindful that your opinions are not always welcome and not everybody appreciates open discussion of their business. Prepare for news and communications to come in thick and fast, with a phone call or e-mail confirming a change in your social plans. It may be time to begin a journey you have been planning for a long time.

Sunday the 25th. Restlessness brings on an eagerness for a change of interests, or a fresh slant on old ones. If you need a spiritual boost, seek out like-minded folks who also want meaning and purpose in their lives. You could put your heads together and do some good work in your community. Don't become entangled in an issue with a neighbor, especially if you know that they are deliberately trying to provoke a response.

Weekly Summary

People can get you down at times. Sometimes dealing with others seems to be too much. Try to be patient and even tempered. A chatty family member who hardly stops long enough to draw breath could grate on your nerves. Even if you cannot get a word in, be kind. Perhaps speaking to you is comforting because of your innate ability to listen without really listening.

On Thursday the Sun enters the expansive sign of Sagittarius, providing good chances to explore new ventures and increase opportunities. This is also a period for lots of activities involving neighbors, relatives, and friends, perhaps kicked off by a happy Thanksgiving feast. Invitations to social gatherings and festive celebrations pour in. Optimism increases with the belief that you can make good luck happen by thinking positive thoughts.

Your thoughts or dreams could leave a permanent impression. Try to remember them so you can write them down. You may need to tighten the purse strings or decide the best way to make your money work for you. If you have had financial problems in the past, seek help from someone who understands how money works. Dress to impress, as you may meet someone very interesting.

48th Week/November 26–December 2

Monday the 26th. Romance is in the air as the early morning favors a quiet romantic interlude. Any new relationship may deepen into a more permanent union. A pleasant time is in store for Aries in love. If you love to cook and display your skills, inviting people for a meal is a delightful way to spend an evening. If you are home alone, watch a romantic film and immerse yourself in the fantasy realm.

Tuesday the 27th. Household matters require attention. If you haven't cleared out a closet for a while, today is the day. You may be amazed at what is lurking in a dark corner. Early evening is a time to compromise with your mate to preserve harmony. A preference to be in a setting close to friends brings comfort and happiness. Ideally, tonight would be suited to curling up on the couch and reveling in domestic bliss.

Wednesday the 28th. The next few days are likely to prove difficult if you are dealing with authority figures. As an Aries you do not take kindly to others issuing orders. Adjust your attitude. Sometimes others do know best. Arrange for help if you are facing a stack of work and are short on time. Aries in writing, publishing, advertising, or sales can expect a busy and successful day.

Thursday the 29th. If social commitments have taken over your life recently, be prepared for loved ones to be annoyed. Distinct signs of jealousy could also emerge and will require an extra display of affection to put things right. Aries searching for a new pastime may find an art group an interesting challenge. This could also help channel creative urges in the right direction.

Friday the 30th. Feelings of lethargy may have a lot to do with the amount of work you must complete prior to the upcoming festivities. You can only do your best. Persuading others to see issues from your point of view can be a breeze if you proceed gently. You won't make much headway if you are too insistent or demanding. Give praise where it is due, especially to children or coworkers.

Saturday December 1st. A nagging sense that something isn't quite right is probably your sixth sense sending a warning. Don't run after others. Do your own thing and you will achieve much. Creative projects will enthuse you and stimulate your energy. Hopeful parents may be expecting a bundle of joy. Your stomach could be more sensitive than usual. Drink some herbal tea and stay away from fatty foods.

Sunday the 2nd. An optimistic attitude can make the impossible happen. But be careful not to make promises you can't keep, which could stretch your stress level to breaking point. A partner can be especially kind and sensitive to your needs. Be responsive, and your sex life can be even more romantic. An interest in the occult can take you a long way from home, so choose your course wisely.

Weekly Summary

Ideas for space saving can make your life easier, cutting the time spent cleaning and looking for things. Make sure you consult your partner about the changes. Otherwise they are likely to be less than friendly. A cooperative effort will make it a lot of fun and give you the opportunity to design a more efficient and individual personal space.

Aries parents to be could be working their way through all the options and opinions on the best method of childbirth. Aries who is not looking forward to a new arrival may be having a similar experience in getting a creative project off the ground. Intuition will be a guiding influence. But take a practical and realistic approach to reach long-term success.

With your ruler Mars retrograde, impetuosity can cause careless actions arising from restlessness. This is a far better time for planning a future project. Write down your ideas, apply for a course to give you needed skills, and start plotting your moves. Work on your physical well-being at the same time, as physical and mental fitness are basic necessities for any endeavor.

49th Week/December 3–9

Monday the 3rd. Leave your personal problems at home this morning. A lot of interesting possibilities lie out there to inspire your thoughts and lift your mood. A legal matter could be preying on your mind, undermining your feelings of personal security. It is important to seek advice from the right person. Do your research and make sure you hire the right adviser.

Tuesday the 4th. A sympathetic rapport between you and your associates will make it easy to influence people to your way of thinking. But don't exaggerate the facts to persuade. It is one thing to argue politics and religion, but talking someone into something they don't want to do will backfire. Infatuation rather than true love could be the driving force behind a new romance.

Wednesday the 5th. Venus, planet of love and harmony, moves into Scorpio today. Venus here will enhance the sexual side of your relationships, adding a touch of intensity. Money can come your way through your business partnerships or a financial institution. A deeper understanding of the issues that underlie your intimate relationships can surface and encourage you to let go of your fears and learn the secret of trust.

Thursday the 6th. Your intuition will be working well, giving you the bargaining skills to get what you want. You may have to draw the line with a loved one. But how to be fair to yourself yet fair to the one you love is stalling your action. Be brave. The key to a happy outcome is honesty and openness. A big night out can have an unsettling effect on the rest of the week. Get plenty of beauty sleep.

Friday the 7th. The cost of your dwelling could be why you are always behind in your bills. Rather than overextending your finances, downsize and move into a place that suits your budget. Paint and special decor can transform the dingy into the bright or small into spacious. Be creative and enjoy having cash to spend. A problem from the past can resurface. Confront whatever it is honestly and resolve it once and for all.

Saturday the 8th. Sun, Moon, Mercury, Jupiter, and Pluto in Sagittarius emphasize higher education and travel. Foreigners and foreign cultures can also figure prominently during the next couple of weeks. Aspiring writers should take this favorable opportunity to approach publishers. They are bound to be interested in your work. Contact friends and relatives who live at a distance and renew your close ties.

Sunday the 9th. Today's New Moon in Sagittarius heralds the beginning of a new and expansive monthly cycle. Big plans and optimism should be the order of the day. Focus on the larger picture of your goals and dreams. Don't get bogged down with the finer details. Your can rely on the help of influential friends. Don't underestimate a belief in magic to guide you along the way. Right now you are only limited by your imagination.

Weekly Summary

Indecision can make you more susceptible to outside influences. Listen to the advice of others but keep a clear picture of your own desired outcomes. Asking for someone else's advice does not mean you are obliged to act on it. Remember that you must meet your own needs, not what someone else thinks you should achieve.

You may not want to be alone early this week. Seek out interaction with others wherever you can find it. It might be a good time to join a group and enjoy a regular social activity without the hassle of going out to find it. A loving relationship can be made more difficult when different views arise on religion and childhood backgrounds.

With your partner you can develop an understanding

and appreciation of each other's differences and promote a foundation of trust from which your love can grow. Generous opportunities appear to come your way later this week. Keep your mind on your goals and choose wisely. Don't take on too much and scatter your energy. Harness it to achieve your main objective.

50th Week/December 10–16

Monday the 10th. Thoughts and ideas tumbling through your mind can distract you from your main purpose. A penchant for practical jokes could put you on the wrong side of someone important. Power struggles are also indicated, and it is imperative that you don't let your emotions take control to the detriment of your ambitions. Remember the adage: Sticks and stones may break my bones, but names will never hurt me.

Tuesday the 11th. A pragmatic approach should return today and give you the staying power to get your work done well. Projects you have left half finished can be completed, giving you a positive sense of achievement. Tackle tasks you put in the too-hard basket and find out how resourceful you really are. Travel plans can become a reality but for a completely different purpose from your original intentions.

Wednesday the 12th. Your present job is probably satisfying but offers little chance for career opportunities. Seek some counsel on the best course of action to branch out and develop your own potential. Inhibitions could be holding you back at the moment. Join a public-speaking group and give your confidence a boost. Contact your parents if you can. Just hearing your voice will give them a lift.

Thursday the 13th. Take a mature approach to relationship difficulties rather than jumping to conclusions or leaving. Get counseling and examine your own actions, not just your partner's. Otherwise you could simply be changing partners to dance to the same tune. Singles should consider involvement in a group to meet people of like mind. You could be pleasantly surprised.

Friday the 14th. Your susceptibility to illness and infection is high. Stay away from sick friends, and don't share eating utensils to be on the safe side. Confusion can be the result of avoidance. Be honest with yourself, and the answer will become clear. A romance could be blossoming with a coworker. Be wise and keep it separate from the workplace.

Saturday the 15th. The need to take a break and get away from your daily routine and responsibilities should be respected. Go away for the weekend. Find a bed-and-breakfast in a secluded and beautiful spot and enjoy the scenery. A spiritual retreat could bring a permanent peace of mind. Friends too will be happy to enjoy your company.

Sunday the 16th. Unexpected visitors may come bearing gifts or offer you a lucrative business deal. A restless spirit could be driving you to do more than you should. It is time to find an outlet for your nervous energy, one that doesn't sap your energy and stir up your emotions. Meditation would be beneficial, even if only for ten minutes a day. Starting a journal can be quite insightful.

Weekly Summary

Political interest can flourish. Whether it is international, national, or local politics, a tendency toward being opinionated is implied. You may hold an influential sway over others at the moment, but try to keep a balanced view in your arguments. If you are part of a debating team, you will be in your element. If you are not, you may want to join one.

Power plays and emotional blackmail may be subtle and underhanded. Look past the obvious to gain more understanding of the intention beneath the action. Secret groups and casual affairs will not do your reputation any good. Keep your actions and alliances aboveboard. Donate your free time to a volunteer organization and reap the rewards that come from making a difference.

Your nerves could be on edge, lowering your tolerance rate to almost nil. Learn a relaxation technique such as meditation and use it on a daily basis. It will help reduce stress levels and eliminate frustration and the risk of losing your cool. An escape from everyday activities might also afford relief. A hobby that doesn't cost much and is easy to do will provide enjoyment without the stress factor.

51st Week/December 17–23

Monday the 17th. An inner conflict between what you want to do and what you feel you should do could make it hard to do anything. Avoid playing the martyr now. It is never rewarding at the best of times. As the day progresses your mood is likely to become more extroverted, and you will be far less sensitive to the moods of others.

Tuesday the 18th. You may ask yourself what you are doing with your life. Consciousness of your goals will be influential, urging you to look at the options open to developing your special skill or calling in life. Act now before it is too late. A shopping trip could turn up a few bargains. In addition, you might run into a casual friend and decide to have a cup of coffee. It might lead to something else.

Wednesday the 19th. Teamwork will achieve far-reaching success today. But be aware of a possible saboteur who will have to be dealt with before such teamwork can happen. A boost in your energy level will make no task too hard. Still, be realistic about what you can and can't do. Get into the fashion swing with a new designer outfit and go out partying tonight.

Thursday the 20th. Juggling your finances can be disheartening at this time of year. Look for gifts that don't cost so much but can be worth more on a sentimental level for a long time. A beautiful poem on a handwritten card, a pressed flower marking a book page, or music that evokes loving memories will be welcomed. Travel plans could present a major setback, sending you back to the drawing board.

Friday the 21st. Difficulties can arise between friends or colleagues because of differing value systems. Find a common ground to come to an agreement. A night out with friends could be too expensive. You can have just as good a time in a cheaper place if you do some looking around. A bonus may be less than you had hoped for, so don't spend it before you get it.

Saturday the 22nd. News from a long-lost friend can make your day. An important celebration could call on you for a speech. No matter how bad your stage fright, you will give a talk that moves your listeners. Arrange for alternate transportation to ensure that you don't drink and drive. You might skip a party to spend a romantic evening with a breathtaking new romance.

Sunday the 23rd. Entertaining at home will be lots of fun. You may have your boss over for a holiday get-together and impress with your talent for catering. Children will come first, and you will want to treat them. If young ones are performing in a show, the proud Aries parent can cheer them on. This evening will be a time for sentiment, remembering the past and those who are no longer with you.

Weekly Summary

The Moon in Aries at the start of this week urges you to treat yourself to a little pampering. Revitalize with a workout at the gym. Or start a personal exercise routine designed to put you in tip-top condition. Reinvent yourself with a new hairstyle, new clothes, and a new attitude. It's time to get the ball rolling and realize what you want. So stop dreaming and start living.

Don't hold yourself back with doubts when the boss singles you out for an important task. Grab the opportunity with both hands and enjoy the experience you are gaining. When it comes to finances, you may be looking forward to having more. But be aware that you need to face your present situation and plan a budget that makes the most of what you have without the need to borrow.

Your kind heart could get the better of you over the weekend, and you might open your home to someone less fortunate. Make sure you set boundaries, or you may end up with a permanent freeloader. Catching up with family and friends who haven't seen or heard from you for a while could occupy your thoughts. Pick up the phone and start calling.

52nd Week/December 24–31

Monday the 24th. A get-together with parents could be fraught with underlying tension, with you and your partner heaving a sigh of relief after they leave. You can both have a good laugh about it afterward and release the tension. A long day at work could infringe on a family outing. Make sure you get there, though. It is better late than never. A public display can be a source of inspiration.

Tuesday the 25th. Merry Christmas! A successful day of festivities is assured. Entertaining at home, although a lot of work, will be rewarding. Seeing the whole clan around the table is cause for celebration in itself. Make sure you get that special someone under the mistletoe. You may have traveled a long way to be with family and to revisit your childhood home. You are content with the rich traditions of your antecedents.

Wednesday the 26th. A long-standing dispute within your family can be settled once and for all, clearing the air for a happier future. A sense of adventure and the simple pure enjoyment of life are indicated. A long journey may be in the works after the holidays. A conversation with a stranger could yield valuable advice, opening up avenues for speculation you hadn't considered before. A contract can be finalized successfully now.

Thursday the 27th. A slow start to the day is advisable. If a hangover is bringing you down, don't be tempted with the hair of the dog. It won't work. Sexual dissatisfaction could be creating tension in your relationship. Don't hide your head in the sand, talk about it. Counseling could also help you sort it out. Problems that are ignored usually tend to grow.

Friday the 28th. A sense of destiny or fate could color everything you do today. You may have to help an elderly relative and can end up listening to their tall tales of adventure. You or your child could land a job with an advertising company, setting a course for a public career. An inheritance may cause dissension in the family but can give you enough to launch a career or business.

Saturday the 29th. Itchy feet and a longing for more variety could be the reasons behind the impulse to move away. A change is as good as a vacation and what begins as a whim could be the best thing you ever did. A public meeting will give you food for thought and could uncover some political dishonesty. The desire to put your strength behind a cause for change can lead you to bigger and better things.

Sunday the 30th. Venus, goddess of love, moves into Sagittarius today and brings an attraction to the arts and travel for the sake of romance and sentiment. As this year comes to a close you might find yourself talking about what you have achieved and what you haven't.

Partnership issues can be discussed lovingly, opening up avenues toward resolution and a healing of old wounds.

Monday the 31st. A reflective mood urges you to do something meaningful for humanity. You might write a letter to the editor, send e-mails to politicians, and visit charity sites on the Internet. A New Year's resolution could be to find out how you can be a more effective citizen of the planet. Your evening is likely to end up in a small gathering with an intimate group of friends.

Weekly Summary

Keeping the home fires burning will be more important than socializing with acquaintances. A desire for a traditional Christmas will override other options. Aries travelers may suffer the pangs of homesickness and even fly home just to be there. Aries parents will want to recreate beloved things from childhood for your own children to experience.

Contact with old faces and childhood memories can bring up all sorts of issues, and not all of them good. Be prepared for disagreements and misunderstandings. But you can also welcome them as a chance to heal past hurts and make peace with those you may have upset or who have upset you. Travel is also indicated, and you could be off on a vacation or visiting family and friends.

As this year comes to a close, you might need to put things in their place, tidy up any loose ends, and start preparing for the New Year in a more methodical and purposeful way than your usual impulsive manner. Old habits do die hard, but the drive to transform negatives into positives will stay with you as you stand up to be counted on your own merits.

DAILY FORECASTS:
JULY–DECEMBER 2006

Saturday July 1st. The tempo of social life is about to increase. Someone you know may need a helping hand but may not confide in you. Cast your eye around your inner circle, as a senior colleague could prove a supportive ally, promoting your interests.

Sunday the 2nd. Family-oriented Aries will have pleasure relaxing and chatting with loved ones and children. Be mindful of health matters. Don't ignore any problems even if slight. Those of you engaging in sporting activities outdoors need to take care.

Monday the 3rd. Activate your imagination today, since you could be inspired to seek an alternative approach. Lunchtime irritability could cause friction with others. Spend this time alone. Home ownership could be of interest, with many Aries achieving this goal.

Tuesday the 4th. Festivities on this Fourth of July offer you the chance to use your natural creative talents. If you are visiting others, make plans early in the day before Mercury goes retrograde. Otherwise, problems with arrangements or travel delays are likely.

Wednesday the 5th. Mercury is now retrograde for the next few weeks, so expect communication mishaps and delays. This influence is not conducive for Aries wishing to seek credit. Watch a tendency to overindulge or do things in excess. Avoid gambling with money or assets.

Thursday the 6th. Mixed trends prevail today. An anticipated social activity may turn out to be a fizzer. Tension surrounding spending joint funds can be avoided if each party is willing to give and take. Aries artists could receive a big break with a sale of a piece of art.

Friday the 7th. Something that you have been wanting could come to you now. Beware of taking on a social commitment that may impinge heavily on your time. Good stars exist for students. Unexpected romantic developments should be to your liking.

Saturday the 8th. A long-distance love affair could gain more permanency now. A weekend retreat could suffice until you can afford a longer vacation. Seek the company of those who are fun loving and with whom you share similar interests. Display your creative talents.

Sunday the 9th. Others could express shock or displeasure by what you say. Patience to overcome obstacles is required. Go for a walk to ease stress. Unpredictable events could throw social plans into disarray, and your love life may not fare much better.

Monday the 10th. New faces on the job bring extra variety to the daily routine. Be receptive to a spur-of-the-moment outing or date. The Capricorn Full Moon brings emotional dramas on the home front. If you want a peaceful night, sneak away to a quiet sanctuary.

Tuesday the 11th. It is an excellent time to formulate long-term career decisions. However, do not implement these until the end of the month. Preferential treatment by someone in authority could lead to further opportunities. This might cause on-the-job jealousy.

Wednesday the 12th. Dependence on a group or organization could be hindering your development. Creativity is stimulated, and an appreciation of beauty and beautiful objects is enhanced now. For some Aries, this could entail purchasing works of art as an investment.

Thursday the 13th. A power struggle with friends or colleagues could surface. Avoid petty squabbles by refusing to be drawn into playing mind games. Conditions from a past situation could arise. Think twice before rushing back into the arms of an old flame.

Friday the 14th. Scheduling meetings during the earlier part of the day will ensure a smoother and more productive flow of discussion. Communication mix-ups and delays still exist. Confirm dinner reservations before leaving home. Romantic attractions are likely passionate and fulfilling but not necessarily long lasting.

Saturday the 15th. Focus on matters of a private nature. Don't commit to social invitations early in the day. Waiting until later should bring more exciting or alternative options. In the romance department, yesterday's influences still exist. Have fun but stick to reality. A new attraction is unlikely to be enduring.

Sunday the 16th. You need action, so don't expect to rest today. A hobby or leisure pursuit that involves physical movement may be the best activity to engage in. Dancing, brisk walking, or swimming could appeal. Switch off jealous or possessive tendencies toward a lover. Otherwise, you may end up alone.

Monday the 17th. A number of minor adjustments to plans could be annoying. Being in the right place at the right time puts you in the position to create your own opportunities. An eye-catching outfit can enhance the wardrobe of the discerning Aries. A tendency to spend freely on family could cause difficulties.

Tuesday the 18th. Money issues in various guises could crop up now. It could be necessary to dip into your savings to cover all outstanding debts. A preoccupation with your own interests could mean you miss something of importance. By looking and listening, you will learn. Good news takes you by surprise.

Wednesday the 19th. With the movement of Venus into the home and family sector of your solar chart, sharing the good times with loved ones will be a priority. Exercise caution with finances, since you may be tempted to buy with your heart rather than your head.

Thursday the 20th. Reconfirm appointments and travel arrangements. Enjoyment comes from chatting with neighbors or others in the local vicinity. Guard against hastily voiced opinions. Check your facts first. You may be misinformed. The physical welfare of an older person could cause some concern.

Friday the 21st. You will be kept busy and on your toes today. An increase in phone, e-mail messages, meetings, and discussions won't provide much time to relax. Contacting service or repair people to organize maintenance on mechanical items can proceed efficiently.

Saturday the 22nd. Sleep late this morning, and you can avoid unpleasantness in the domestic arena. If you do become drawn into the fray, avert further friction by choosing your words carefully. You might be inclined to say the wrong thing. Rental tenants who need repairs should find landlords quick to respond.

Sunday the 23rd. Activity abounds now with the Sun in Leo in your solar fifth house and Mars in Virgo in your solar sixth house. While you will still want lots of fun activities, your attention will also move toward work and health matters. New job prospects could be presented, providing better pay and conditions.

Monday the 24th. The Leo New Moon occurring in your house of creativity can bring praise and recognition for the artistic Aries. Family help could aid those of you currently looking to upgrade employment conditions. Home improvements begun now should produce great results. Profound insight may be life changing.

Tuesday the 25th. There may be no quick solution to an ongoing problem. Only time may provide the answer. Protecting joint resources could be of concern. Don't take anything for granted, but look for alternatives. Children's activities and interests come to the fore. A family member could make a happy announcement.

Wednesday the 26th. You may be asked to take a leadership role or make important decisions. Work or family responsibilities could interfere with plans for a social gathering. Try to be objective and avoid an emotional reaction. Prolonged aggravation can affect your health. Be wary about lending money to friends.

Thursday the 27th. Enhancement of fitness levels continues if exercise regimens are adhered to. Working alone can alleviate frustration. A business meeting might be a test of your personal credibility. Play it cool, and you should come out on top. Improvements to domestic surroundings can be implemented.

Friday the 28th. Health, diet, work, and domestic concerns could demand that you to rearrange your schedule. Fulfilling a commitment of an emotional nature may take priority. If you are seeking employment, a confidential approach could produce results. Socially, an outing with an artistic flavor could please.

Saturday the 29th. Health problems this morning could be linked to an overabundance of the good life. Excessive indulgence in food and alcohol could be the cause of a stomach upset or digestive problems. Take advantage of interesting invitations. Good vibes exist for Aries looking for a new intimate relationship.

Sunday the 30th. You could find a willingness to try new things, even if you're uncertain of the outcome. Opportunities exist to show your true colors and how competent you are. Observe what is happening, and you can learn about your own and others' capabilities.

Monday the 31st. Proceed slowly if a relationship problem arises today. Impulsive actions or words could add fuel to the fire, making matters worse. Perhaps your partner is feeling jealous, left out, or unloved. Do your best to revitalize intimacy, and closeness should follow. Concentrate on what unites rather than separates.

Tuesday August 1st. Reevaluate domestic circumstances and implement changes. The home refurbishing that is on your list of tasks to do can be acted upon now. Be original, and you will be more than pleased with the results. Take extra care filling out forms relating to finances. Double-check that everything is in order.

Wednesday the 2nd. Lady Luck is not looking your way today. Avoid areas where you could be tempted to risk money. Be careful that you don't arouse or inflame family hostility. A partner or loved one could be moody. When leaving the house or apartment, double-check that all security measures have been taken.

Thursday the 3rd. On the home front it could be out with the old and in with the new for remodeling. Share your thoughts, feelings, and aspirations with loved ones. If these are impractical, it is better to find out now so that realistic aims can be put into place. Inspiration can come if you think outside the box.

Friday the 4th. Writer's block suppresses creative output this morning. Find another task to do until later on in the day when motivation and bright ideas again flow freely. Teenagers endeavoring to choose a profession or a college could find the task easier today. Camaraderie can be found within a therapy or self-help group.

Saturday the 5th. Someone new could inspire you with his or her talent and artistic ability. This could give you the impetus to abandon the tried and tested. Create your own individual style with everything you touch. Don't let others bully you into spending over the budget. A former lover could reignite an old passion.

Sunday the 6th. Mutual benefits could come through friends. Opportunities to bring about changes, resolve differences, or deepen a relationship abound. If a proposition is presented now, brainstorm with trusted family or friends before going further.

Monday the 7th. Professional prospects look brighter than personal affairs today. On-the-job abilities can bring you into prominence. Dealings with the public should flow easily. Finish whatever projects are nearing completion before tackling anything else. At home, extra work may strain your circulatory system.

Tuesday the 8th. An application to join an elite or professional club should be well received. Harmonious relations with loved ones can come by balancing the time spent on the job with time spent at home. Possible problems associated with an inheritance might surface. Getting enough exercise will be important to your physical well-being.

Wednesday the 9th. Influences from the Full Moon could impel risk taking, so remain cautious. However, it won't do any harm to pursue a long-term plan. Assess the commitment before making binding decisions. Try to strengthen a faltering relationship.

Thursday the 10th. Take one step at a time today. Pace yourself so that your vitality is not strained. Trying to touch too many bases at once can result in a deadlock. Avoid intervening in a workplace dispute. Instead, watch to see how the situation unravels. Venturing out alone is not recommended this evening.

Friday the 11th. Mercury is now residing in Leo, your house of love and leisure, so expect new developments in this area. Aries can be accident-prone. It would be wise to watch your step. Someone may prefer to be left alone. Stay clear and respect the feelings of another.

Saturday the 12th. With Venus now also in Leo, watch your diet. Sensitivity or intolerance to rich food or alcohol could cause an allergic reaction. Embarking on a course of self-development or self-empowerment can be gratifying. An added benefit could be your less aggressive attitude and improved self-confidence.

Sunday the 13th. A planetary emphasis on love and personal relationships brings significance to your romantic life. Many Aries could fall in love for the first time. For couples pondering the future of a current love affair, a turning point may be drawing closer. A little windfall may come along for the lucky among you. Someone you have been counting on may let you down.

Monday the 14th. Give shopping a wide berth. Avoidance of tasks today will mean an increased workload tomorrow. Give a coworker the benefit of the doubt. Perhaps there is a legitimate reason. Sincerity can assist in resolving relationship problems.

Tuesday the 15th. Finding out the hard way that your bank account is overdrawn or not as flush as you thought could bring dissension with a partner. Perhaps it is time to sort out financial details and organize a fairer distribution of funds. A social occasion is likely to do wonders for your self-confidence.

Wednesday the 16th. You should make a good impression on most people who cross your path today. Networking is important, so cultivate a valuable contact. Even if you do not like the advice given by others, look interested. There may be many pearls of wisdom among the rhetoric.

Thursday the 17th. Financial negotiations could center on a small detail that needs to be resolved before moving forward. Social activities should be enjoyable this evening. Be on guard and don't engage in gossip or talk too much if you are mixing with colleagues.

Friday the 18th. Avoid strained relations by being extra tactful around midmorning. You could slip up and then realize you have made a serious blunder or divulged too much information. Unexpected visitors could put a strain on relationships and the household budget. Be honest and let others know if you are unable to cope.

Saturday the 19th. To reduce the risk of cuts or burns, take extra care when handling sharp or hot objects. Purchasing a special gift for a loved one conveys a sense of satisfaction. Don't spoil it by spending more than you can afford and then worrying about it later.

Sunday the 20th. Work requiring methodical application can progress smoothly. A delicate family issue may be no closer to a resolution. Old wounds take time to heal. It may be best to let the issue rest. Someone's departure could be upsetting. A change of scenery later in the day can be rejuvenating.

Monday the 21st. There seem to be adverse influences concerning health and work. Stress or nervous tension could cause minor hearing or speech problems. Absent colleagues might mean that you are stuck with extra work. Take precautions, as your chances of being misled or deceived are increased now.

Tuesday the 22nd. Someone close could develop selective hearing. Give up. He or she probably does not want to hear what you have to say. Youngsters may be determined to keep parents on the go. Feelings of being bombarded with more than you can handle are likely. Defer tasks that require exact attention to detail.

Wednesday the 23rd. If you have not achieved what you set out to do over the past few days, now is the opportune time to catch up. Avoid procrastinating and get on with it. Your attitude may be narrower than usual, but this will allow a much more focused approach. A loved one could need your support and strength.

Thursday the 24th. Deceptive influences are at work today. Be prepared, Aries. Verify your facts first before speaking out. A perfectionist attitude is the likely cause of relationship tension. Singles looking for a long-term commitment may need to come down from the clouds and be realistic. Love may be closer to home.

Friday the 25th. Displaying impulsiveness or rash behavior could upset others. However, staying cool, calm, and in control may be a challenge for forthright Aries. Despite careful planning, a long-awaited social activity may disappoint. Pay attention to health problems.

Saturday the 26th. Volunteering your assistance for a children's support or youth program could bring fulfillment and a sense of satisfaction. This is not a good day to stretch your luck too far. A loved one may be draining emotional and financial resources. Call a halt.

Sunday the 27th. Reevaluate recent decisions, since a better alternative could be available. Couples who are experiencing problems communicating feelings to each other might need to examine the relationship. A new love affair that begins now should be long lasting.

Monday the 28th. Changes to your day-to-day routine, although exhausting, will be productive. You also welcome the diversity. Vague plans need clarification. Networking for social or business purposes can further your progress. Let a partner take the lead.

Tuesday the 29th. Target what needs to be acted on first. A highly informative and useful encounter with a group could bring a sense of relief. Passions are easily aroused now. If you make a connection with a romantic interest, make sure it is for the right reasons.

Wednesday the 30th. Complicated plans need to be reorganized. Drive with care. Other drivers might be inclined to road rage. Try to recognize the warning signs from your body. An inability to control touchiness may be an indication that rest is needed.

Thursday the 31st. Before taking off for parts unknown, make sure that others have a copy of your travel itinerary. As an added safety measure, call home on a regular basis. Foreign interests could bring benefits for those of you in business. Dissension with in-laws or an old family feud could erupt. Keeping quiet will be best.

Friday September 1st. Inspiration and ideas flow freely today. Aries on vacation could enjoy a romantic liaison with an attractive fellow traveler. Sharing your knowledge and wisdom will be appreciated. A hobby or favored pastime could progress into a small business.

Saturday the 2nd. Aries organizational skills are enhanced. If tension exists, do as much as possible to restore rapport with others. Promotion of creative projects is likely to generate increased income. Recognition for past efforts could be forthcoming.

Sunday the 3rd. A delayed project may gain momentum. The wheels have been set in motion for something significant to come about. A misinterpreted statement or gesture could fuel an altercation. Current influences are excellent for a long journey to further career advancement. A sport or physical activity might be the perfect outlet for your competitive nature.

Monday the 4th. Children and their interests are favorably accented. How and where you earn your living could claim the attention of some Aries. Shop for home appliances before noon. Friends could prove problematic. Even if you are not inclined to, there may be no other choice than to deal with their issues.

Tuesday the 5th. Monotonous work can frustrate even those Aries who don't mind routine. A know-it-all attitude could cause an argument. You may need to concede that you don't have all the answers. Domestic squabbles or clashes could prove tiresome. A friend could cancel out at the last minute.

Wednesday the 6th. Venus is now residing in the sign of Virgo in your solar sixth house of daily life, work, and health. Professional duties may require persistence and ingenuity. Changes to your diet, a weekly visit to the gym, or a daily walk are measures that can improve well-being. Mystical activities could attract.

Thursday the 7th. The Full Moon in the sign of Pisces in your solar twelfth house could bring annoying delays or mishaps. Just grin and bear it. Old grievances could bring complications. Read the fine print before committing to any transactions. Behind-the-scenes activities require a cautious approach.

Friday the 8th. Your ruling planet Mars is now in your solar seventh house and your opposite sign of Libra for a monthlong visit. This could bring up issues about where your relationship is headed and your own needs. Intervention in disputes among colleagues may be necessary. Step lightly to avoid further conflict.

Saturday the 9th. You are moving closer now to realizing your objectives. Stretch your limits and assert yourself. Being passionate about personal matters can lead to impulsive action. Your ability to understand and assimilate concepts is enhanced. This an excellent time to begin or continue studies relating to the human psyche.

Sunday the 10th. Sound financial judgment aids an ability to see the value in material goods. If you need to make purchases for the home, you are unlikely to overspend now. Party plans make progress. Socializing could stimulate interesting business concepts.

Monday the 11th. Current planetary influences indicate that complex monetary issues may need to be sorted out. Accumulated partnership expenses are worrisome. Unpredictable investments could result in losses. Avoid a risk venture. Your leadership skills may be in demand. Coworkers seek your companionship.

Tuesday the 12th. All sorts of financial opportunities could be presented. Signing of contracts, legal matters, and business propositions should move ahead with little effort. It may not be appealing now to try and motivate others. Concentrate on what you consider important for personal happiness. Spend within your means.

Wednesday the 13th. Aries on the lookout for a new job could hear news to your advantage. Others are likely to agree with your ideas but could be noncommittal and defer making a decision. Inspiration is enhanced, so let your imagination guide you to creating something wonderful. Meet and mix with local friends or neighbors.

Thursday the 14th. Loved ones may accuse you of being more interested in work than family life. Take extra precautions when signing personal or business leases. Find out the reason why previous tenants vacated the premises.

Friday the 15th. Someone close could have a short fuse today. Keep the peace by holding back on angry retorts. Influences are not conducive for property purchases. Problems that are not immediately obvious could arise. Don't try and fix any equipment yourself. Have an expert repair it or purchase new items.

Saturday the 16th. Domestic concerns demand close attention. A new relationship may be exotic and unusual, although possibly short-lived. A much-loved animal could cause you some anxiety. Artistic ideas may be expressed through redecorating.

Sunday the 17th. A new baby or in-law could add to the family circle. Parents may have reason to celebrate a child's endeavors. Financial support of youngsters' plans or aims can provide invaluable experiences and prospects for future employment. If romance is a priority, look forward to an enjoyable evening.

Monday the 18th. Demanding family commitments could slow you down. Special opportunities could be within the reach of Aries with distinctive skills and expertise. Competent efforts and quick service enhance your reputation and can carve out a niche for you in the marketplace. Discontent in a romance could be because of unrealistic expectations.

Tuesday the 19th. A breakfast meeting could be profitable. A youngster may demand attention or need extra love and care. Someone could stretch the truth. Idiosyncrasies of others may prove bothersome. Creativity and romance are favored, with some of you announcing an engagement or a proposal.

Wednesday the 20th. Motivation to improve your physical condition and lifestyle could be strong. Changing conditions on the job may be affecting your home and family life. Finding a balance between the two may be complicated but is manageable.

Thursday the 21st. Streamlining and organizing current work patterns allow for greater output today. Fluctuations in sales could be worrisome for retail owners. Finding love in the workplace is a possibility. Confirm that money invested on your behalf in an insurance or pension plan is producing expected results.

Friday the 22nd. Apply caution in matters relating to joint funds or investments. Something you choose to disregard could become troublesome. It may be wise to take action now rather than later when the problem could be far worse. Changes in your domestic environment are likely. Someone may move out or move in.

Saturday the 23rd. The Sun is now residing in the sign of Libra, along with Mercury and Mars, emphasizing the relationships sector in your solar chart. An opportunity now exists to improve relations. Be prepared and willing to compromise and make concessions. An unexpected situation could give you a jolt.

Sunday the 24th. Refrain from in-depth discussion on a topic of which you have little understanding. An outstanding debt may be creating emotional strain. There is a way around any limitations, so think of solutions rather than stressing out. A new romantic relationship could become more significant and transforming.

Monday the 25th. Learn lessons from past mistakes and faults, but avoid worrying about situations that cannot be changed. Ensure that all insurance policies are adequate and paid in advance. A secret meeting could be a combination of business, pleasure, and romance.

Tuesday the 26th. Hasty action may cause a minor accident around the home or office. Keep a tight control on all financial affairs and especially anticipated joint income. A reshuffle in the work environment could take you by surprise. Complying with grace to short-term disadvantages could eventually bring long-term gains. People you have lost contact with could reappear.

Wednesday the 27th. A positive outlook can attract luck. With good fortune flowing, a game of chance could increase the bank balance. There may be happy news regarding a planned social activity or upcoming vacation. Relatives who reside overseas could come to visit.

Thursday the 28th. Problems could arise for those of you on vacation. Express your dissatisfaction assertively unless these are of your own making. If lack of money is the reason, the situation could accelerate. An invitation to a happy occasion might arrive in the mail. Learning a new skill could lead to career promotion.

Friday the 29th. Watch out for a coworker who could attempt to take credit for your efforts. Settlement of property through divorce or separation could proceed with mostly favorable results. Guard against pushing yourself too hard, as your expectations may be too high. Slow down and take time out for recreation.

Saturday the 30th. Demanding tasks may require an innovative approach. Goal-oriented Aries could be presented to the public through a special project. Sparks could fly with a partner. Indecision is the possible cause of tension. A social setting might be the place for a family feud to reignite.

Sunday October 1st. Don't believe everything others have to say today. Even the most knowledgeable can be wrong occasionally. Check all information before taking any action. Reassessing new career opportunities and resources could be a step in the right direction.

Monday the 2nd. Jointly held money, tax requirements, estate matters, and insurance coverage require more attention. Benefits come through cooperating, understanding, and working in association with others. Guard against intolerance or a critical attitude.

Tuesday the 3rd. Resist pressure from others to act spontaneously. A decision made on the spur of the moment is unlikely to be a wise move. Friends and social responsibilities may put a strain on the budget. Pay your own way if going out, even with your partner.

Wednesday the 4th. A display of stubbornness could irritate others. Closely check any offers made. Someone else could gain more benefits than you will. Socializing could be more of a bother that it's worth. With vitality at a low ebb, it may be better to catch up on sleep.

Thursday the 5th. Performing daily routine tasks could take a supreme effort. Try and find something interesting to do that can help relieve the boredom. The health of a partner or loved one could be a concern. Conducting research in private could be advantageous.

Friday the 6th. The Full Moon brings an opportunity to move ahead with pet projects. Cooperating with others could test your patience. Personal matters come to the fore. If it has been some time since you altered your image, perhaps it is time to change your hairstyle.

Saturday the 7th. Your enthusiastic attitude is likely to have a remarkable effect. If you need financial backing for personal projects, others should quickly agree to your terms. Personal and physical changes can be implemented now. Give more thought to an ongoing issue.

Sunday the 8th. Watch your checkbook if venturing out to the stores. Be prudent. Luxury purchases may have visual appeal without any practical application. Concentration could be difficult later in the day. If events start to get on top of you or you become emotional, release your feelings in a positive manner.

Monday the 9th. Applying ingenuity at work should please those of you in authority. Don't leave valuables unattended or carry large amounts of cash without an escort. Expenses that you did not anticipate could arrive in the mail. There may be compelling reasons why a review of past mistakes will be necessary.

Tuesday the 10th. The ability to add a personal touch enhances work requiring originality. Valuable items could be misplaced. Takes measures so that you can remember where you place things. Something unexpected could require a change in plans. Those of you who are unattached could find a romantic interest.

Wednesday the 11th. Exchange of ideas and information can produce benefits. There could be interesting news regarding a social event or a weekend getaway plan. For Aries gardeners, this is a favorable day. Neighborhood resources might prove to be invaluable. A lively social life contributes to love and romance.

Thursday the 12th. Don't expect everything to fall easily into place today. If you are seeking peace and quiet on the home front, you will need to differentiate between work and socializing. Energy will be focused on home responsibilities this evening.

Friday the 13th. Enjoy social activities that are inexpensive but fun. Replacing household appliances could diminish any recent savings made in the domestic budget. Family issues would benefit if members are encouraged to speak candidly of current concerns. Open discussions can clear the air, allowing adjustments to be made.

Saturday the 14th. Don't underestimate the potential of your creative ideas and skills. Improved earnings could come from producing and selling original designs. Allow enough time to get yourself and your services known. Show off your domestic or culinary skills, Aries. Invite those you want to impress for a formal dinner party.

Sunday the 15th. There is an emphasis on the younger members of the family. A pregnancy or the birth of a baby may be cause for celebration. Or someone could move out of the family home, perhaps for the first time. This could cause mixed feelings.

Monday the 16th. Monday-morning blues are likely to strike some of you. You may not have the opportunity to give into these feelings, as others could be relying on your organizational skills and expertise. A social phase begins now. A new friendship will need time to develop. Young Aries could be pleasantly surprised by the ideas of the older generation.

Tuesday the 17th. Personal distractions could divert your attention from daily duties and work responsibilities. It may be next to impossible trying to please everyone in the family. At least try to please your partner. Double-check the bill if dining out.

Wednesday the 18th. Employment prospects are improved for Aries currently seeking to rejoin the workforce or move on to greener pastures. Any propensity to argue with others should be carefully restrained. Under current influences, organizing and taking care of details can benefit. However, guard against overanalyzing.

Thursday the 19th. If you are sure of your facts, figures, or answers, go straight to the point. Self-confidence and enthusiasm shine through. For those of you attending a job interview or important meeting, apply the charm and you should impress. You probably won't mind what you do today as long as other people are around.

Friday the 20th. A busy and productive day lies ahead. It is time to get physical with work and play, so roll up your sleeves and tackle whatever needs to be done. Many Aries will be anxious to go out and party. Couples may prefer to spend quality time alone.

Saturday the 21st. Decisions are likely if an emotional issue is discussed with family members honestly and with integrity. A windfall could catch you or your lover by surprise. Creativity can present opportunities. Aries living at home or sharing with others may need to make adjustments to behavior and honor house rules.

Sunday the 22nd. The Libra New Moon today offers an opportunity to take a fresh look at your relationships. Changes can be successfully implemented to further enhance a happy union or to add zeal to one that lacks tolerance and joy. Watch your step, as you are accident-prone. Walk, don't run, and do one thing at a time.

Monday the 23rd. With the Sun and Mars in Scorpio, you could be infused with a spirit of adventure and daring. Don't go overboard, Aries. A lack of clear thinking could impel risk-taking activities. Intense emotional energy could thrust you into judging others too harshly. Think about what you want and why.

Tuesday the 24th. Venus has now joined the Sun, Mercury, Mars, and Jupiter in the passionate sign of Scorpio. This planetary emphasis brings focus to all financial matters, particularly jointly owned assets and money. A renewed sense of intimacy can bring closeness and added spice to relationships.

Wednesday the 25th. Be willing to give a little. A philosophical attitude could help. When everything appears to be falling apart, it could be just a matter of timing. Perhaps you are doing the right thing at the wrong time. A meditation session has benefits. Favorable stars exist for love, romance, and intimate relationships.

Thursday the 26th. Try to achieve your aims early, as current planetary influences could deplete energy. Rely on intuition, and pay attention to what your body is telling you. Watch for signs of tiredness and take appropriate action. Rest, relax, and restore your well-being. Overseas travel could beckon the adventurous Aries.

Friday the 27th. Consider where you are in terms of career. For those of you who are not yet where you want to be or are not moving in the right direction, it may be time to make changes. Don't tell little white lies. If you are unable or don't want to do what is asked, be up front and say so. Socializing may lack the usual sparkle.

Saturday the 28th. Mercury is now in retrograde motion. Over the next three weeks, areas of your life dealing with communication, siblings, and travel will be affected by niggling little delays, errors, and misunderstandings. It is not an auspicious period to start anything new or to lay out large sums of money on a house, car, or boat. This is a time for closure.

Sunday the 29th. Overcoming strained relations may be difficult but not entirely impossible. Recognize that at present there is a great deal of intensity surrounding intimate relationships. Avoid becoming upset over minor incidents. You may discover a talent for music or an artistic ability that has up to now been dormant.

Monday the 30th. If you haven't enough funds to pay outstanding expenses, approach a friend for a short-term loan. Getting on with the job will require patience, imagination, and the right timing. Look at creative methods if established techniques don't measure up.

Tuesday the 31st. Remove useless clutter from your home and office. Scrutinize all information before passing it on. Showering love and affection on family and partners will be appreciated by them. The intensity of passionate feelings could surprise even fiery Aries.

Wednesday November 1st. Current planetary influences assist Aries to learn more about the stock market or financial trading. Now is the time to take steps to secure your finances and income potential. Behind-the-scenes activities or private research should produce promising results. Preserve confidential information.

Thursday the 2nd. This is another favorable day where financial resources are concerned. Tension in the air warns against making any impulsive domestic or career decisions. Slowly assimilate information before taking action. Care is needed with a woman within your social circle who shows envious behavior.

Friday the 3rd. Clarify goals and future hopes before moving forward with joint ventures. Business operators gain advantages by supplying prompt and competent work and service. You may prefer to be left to your own devices. Time spent indulging an artistic passion can be invigorating. Push yourself harder than usual.

Saturday the 4th. Economic factors may need consideration, especially those involving a partnership. Keeping a cool head can assist in avoiding unnecessary arguments regarding your current financial position. Some of you could receive a lovely gift, a sentimental memento, or a family heirloom.

Sunday the 5th. Issues involving joint finances persist. The influence of the Full Moon heightens sensitivity to slights either real or figments of your imagination. Arguments with others are likely. If you don't want to spoil your whole day, steer clear of topics or people that annoy you. Plan a budget that allows saving for the future.

Monday the 6th. An unexpected expense or a current cash-flow crisis could see many Aries frantically trying to borrow much-needed funds. It would be wise to remember the old saying, more haste less speed. If driving, take care and obey the road rules.

Tuesday the 7th. Keep in contact with neighbors, as they may have important information to share. Today favors scheduling meetings, conferences, or arranging job interviews. Negotiating better wages and conditions should also prove fruitful if conducted during the morning hours. Later, messages could be confusing.

Wednesday the 8th. Changes within the domestic environment or family situation are likely. A fact or idea you have can be turned into a personal or professional advantage. At home check that windows and doors are securely locked against possible intruders.

Thursday the 9th. Your ability to get things moving will be appreciated by others in your circle. Eloquence in speech is good for Aries to present a sales pitch, prepared lecture, or off-the-cuff address. Additions to assets could come through someone giving you a family heirloom or from a purchase of a collector's item.

Friday the 10th. A family project is about to come to a successful conclusion. You could instinctively know what is likely to bring future monetary gains. Aries into sports could be on the winning side. A hobby or creative pastime brings pleasure to those at home. Launching a home-based venture is auspicious now.

Saturday the 11th. The tendency to act in haste and often with little thought is characteristic of Aries. Stop and listen to what others have to say. Many of you will be more intent on concentrating on creative or artistic endeavors than socializing. An invitation for a wedding or christening could bring family excitement.

Sunday the 12th. Support could be withdrawn for one of your pet projects. Later on there may be a change of heart, so don't give up just yet. Children can require special guidance. A short journey with a loved one could add pleasure to the day. Put excess energy into plans for entertaining guests.

Monday the 13th. A number of obstacles will need to be overcome at work. Don't drive yourself too hard in order to finish all the tasks. Spreading duties over the day will make it easier. Set priorities and reduce pressure. Collecting money owed can proceed hassle free. A disturbing secret worry can be sorted out now.

Tuesday the 14th. Something that ends or changes today could bring unsettling conditions. You may not be at all pleased with these new circumstances. A task you keep postponing should·be easier to manage. Be tactful and show consideration to fellow workers without allowing them to take up too much of your time. Overindulgence could see you go off a health regimen.

Wednesday the 15th. An ability to manage and delegate duties without upsetting others will please your boss. Pent-up emotions and energy could be poured into physical activities. The client base should grow for Aries currently in business. Parents, teachers, or caregivers may encounter problems with children.

Thursday the 16th. Watch your step today, Aries. Minor mishaps are likely, so put your personal safety above all other considerations. Working together as a team with your partner can assist in paying financial obligations. Someone you respect and admire may act as a mentor.

Friday the 17th. The tempo of social activities is about to increase. Understand where others are coming from before making rash judgments or statements. Take care to explain your words or actions if someone misinterprets what you say or do. Knowing your legal rights or obligations could assist with a decision.

Saturday the 18th. With Mercury now moving forward, the likelihood of delays, lost or misplaced paperwork, and computer problems should be greatly reduced. Contracts can be signed with more confidence. Landlords could find the right tenant to rent a house.

Sunday the 19th. Becoming embroiled in other people's affairs or arguments could result in someone leaving on bad terms. Try to arrange an outing or activity that brings excitement and happiness. Stay away from any type of gambling activities, including the lottery.

Monday the 20th. The New Moon in Scorpio presents an opportunity to rethink the way you do things. If changes are needed, these can now be implemented. A tricky situation with a former lover could bring slight unease. This is a good day to take a calculated risk, as long as you have the knowledge and know-how.

Tuesday the 21st. Exciting projects at your workplace could bring you an opportunity to showcase your potential and achieve. Matters that may have caused past difficulties will seem easier and quite simple. It is a favorable period to begin a new study or training course. A special travel goal may be more achievable now.

Wednesday the 22nd. The Sun is now transiting Sagittarius in your solar ninth house until December 22nd. This is an opportune time to enhance your knowledge and upgrade employment skills. A troublesome situation could be resolved if concessions are made. Benefits come through writing, publishing, or travel.

Thursday the 23rd. This Thanksgiving holiday is likely to be special. Old friends or loved ones will enjoy festivities with you, as you reminisce about past holidays and shared joys. A boost in your love life is a possibility. Don't let a show of temper from someone spoil what otherwise will be a great day.

Friday the 24th. There are lucky stars shining on you now that Jupiter, the planet of good fortune, has moved into the sign of Sagittarius. Unexpected good news may be related to a vacation involving overseas travel. By showing responsibility, motivation, and drive, all those in authority will take notice.

Saturday the 25th. You may be obliged to alter today's activities. Others could be upset because they were not asked to be included in your original plans. This is a favorable day for Aries involved in a political movement. Be choosy about the company you keep this evening.

Sunday the 26th. Contacts from the past could prove helpful with arranging an overseas vacation. Try and keep plans to yourself until you are nearly ready to act. Others are not as farsighted as you are and may cause disruptions. Making a decision regarding a friendship could prove difficult.

Monday the 27th. Avoid taking unnecessary risks, especially if you are participating in an adventure trip. Don't be surprised if a friend or associate wants to borrow money. However, saying no may jeopardize the friendship. If you have offered to help a relative with a move, honor your word.

Tuesday the 28th. You could indulge a natural urge to show sympathy and understanding toward others. Care is needed that this compassion is not misdirected. Otherwise, you could end up in a compromising entanglement. This is a good day to clear your house of clutter and remove articles that are taking up space.

Wednesday the 29th. The Moon in your own sign of Aries conveys extra drive and determination. A personal plan could become complex. On the job, a responsibility allocated to you can draw attention to your expertise, providing a career boost. Get an early start if traveling long distances.

Thursday the 30th. Career-minded Aries could see that your current wardrobe and your beauty regimen meet appropriate standards. If it is essential to dress in a professional manner, make time for some serious shopping. To obtain the best results, do things in a straightforward manner today.

Friday December 1st. A flexible schedule is needed to accommodate possible interruptions or minor mix-ups today. Also, a variety of activities or errands could keep you hopping. Computer breakdowns, banking errors, or faults with other technology might be the cause of delays in accessing money or paying bills. If socializing, don't leave personal possessions unattended.

Saturday the 2nd. Financial considerations may overshadow social plans. Regardless of how tempting these may be, the actual cost will need to be carefully calculated. If possible, avoid traveling long distances. Solutions to any problems can come from looking at a situation from a different perspective.

Sunday the 3rd. Today will have its ups and downs. Laying out money for items other than basic family necessities could stretch the household finances. Confirm any news or rumors heard now. Find the truth of the matter before action is taken.

Monday the 4th. Emotions are likely to be quickly aroused from the influences of today's Full Moon. This is not a very good day to make decisions regarding current living arrangements. If possible, avoid home entertaining, as too many things could go wrong. There may not be much happening on the romantic scene.

Tuesday the 5th. Benefits can come if time is spent catching up on correspondence. Problems could be discovered regarding a contract or a lease. If you handle this type of document, make sure it is error free. You don't want to be blamed for mistakes.

Wednesday the 6th. Disruptions are likely. Visitors could turn up unannounced. Make sure the housework is up-to-date and the cupboards well stocked. A culturally inspired social activity creates a happy sense of well-being. Mars moving into Sagittarius today brings a boost of energy and enthusiasm.

Thursday the 7th. Preparing for weekend guests could see many of you shopping. You may have overlooked some very important items. Pursue your creative ideas, especially if you intend to make rather than buy Christmas gifts. Others will appreciate your thoughtfulness.

Friday the 8th. The Sun and Venus, Pluto, Jupiter, and Mars all now occupy your solar ninth house. These influences can broaden horizons and expand consciousness, two areas where your energy can be focused. Although honesty is the best policy, you may need to take a diplomatic approach to questions asked. Think before responding so that problems can be avoided.

Saturday the 9th. Home and family activities benefit from creative ideas and input. Long-distance communications or upcoming travel arrangements require attention. Social plans could be altered. Confirm arrangements before leaving home. Unanswered romantic questions may be the cause of confusion for many of you.

Sunday the 10th. An exchange of words is likely, although a situation should be resolved quickly and then forgotten. Don't overlook health issues. If problems, however minor, persist, consult a doctor. It is advisable to rest. Too much socializing, visiting, or entertaining could be physically draining.

Monday the 11th. Venus is now residing in the thrifty sign of Capricorn. Tasks that have been neglected because no one was willing to do them before can now begin. Do-it-yourself tasks are favored for Aries who are handy with their hands. You could be reminded that a dental or medical checkup has not been followed up.

Tuesday the 12th. You could feel an urge to make changes to improve your physical health and wellness. Judgment is on target now for those of you who are inclined to invest or speculate in areas with minimum risks. Success is likely in a business development.

Wednesday the 13th. Aries does like to be fancy-free, without too many restrictions. You may need to advise another that your freedom and independence are important to you. However, make sure you grant your partner the same liberty that you expect from him or her. A business partnership may run into difficulties. Compromise might only bring a short-term solution.

Thursday the 14th. An exciting event could bring public recognition for some Aries. However, not everyone in your social circle will be thrilled for you. A productive day is ahead for those in creative fields. Make the most of inspirational and imaginative ideas.

Friday the 15th. Friendships could be a source of difficulties today. You may need to counsel others or ask them to calm down and keep control of their emotions. On the job, this is a good time for Aries in charge to remove any waste or mismanagement. However, don't try to implement new methods until after the New Year. Couples should be on the same romantic wavelength.

Saturday the 16th. You are proud of your home and could spend the morning planning changes in your furnishings. Your thoughtfulness and kindness will be appreciated by an elderly relative. If you are single and looking for love, don't be pushy. Coming on too strong could scare off any interested party.

Sunday the 17th. An out-of-town relative or friend of your roommate could be of romantic interest. If you are looking for action and variety, try visiting new locations. Or a movie featuring scenes of famous sites and cultural monuments could appeal.

Monday the 18th. Job problems as well as your workload could be building to a climax. If an expedient solution is not found, further complications are possible. Don't be disappointed if you don't get along with everyone you meet on the social scene.

Tuesday the 19th. Receipt of important news or a development that leads to achieving a goal could create excitement. Using creativity and applying a unique twist can bring accolades as well as extra income. Use a touch of humility if seeking an increase in salary. Entertaining guests at home this evening brings pleasure.

Wednesday the 20th. The New Moon in Sagittarius activates the sector of your Aries solar chart that deals with the acquisition of knowledge. Make the most of opportunities, as this new cycle can bring exciting prospects that promote ambition. Writers, salespeople, and teachers can receive extra benefits.

Thursday the 21st. Shop for gifts around midmorning. Selection should be easier with plenty of choices available. If you haven't completed everything, leave the rest until tomorrow. You could be an accident waiting to happen if you continue to rush around after dark. Give yourself a breather. Take time out.

Friday the 22nd. With the Sun now residing in ambitious Capricorn, any troubling issues surrounding employment should start to clear. Meetings with those in authority who can assist professional goals should bring pleasing results. For some Aries, a significant development could be the start of a new life-altering phase.

Saturday the 23rd. A group activity should be stimulating and revealing. Spur-of-the-moment travel plans are unlikely to be welcomed. Work-related matters could be the reason for travel rather than an exciting holiday vacation. The extravagance of a loved one could bring stress. A new love prospect might make an appearance.

Sunday the 24th. Problems that have confounded you in the past may be easily resolved now. Examine old issues for an answer. Indulge yourself tonight and get into the holiday spirit. Sing carols, attend a midnight church service, or circulate among favorite companions.

Monday the 25th. Merry Christmas! The setting for to-day's celebrations can contribute to your happiness and joy. Lots of excitement should fill your home, along with family, friends, and close neighbors. The religious and spiritual aspect of this day will be emphasized.

Tuesday the 26th. If you stayed up to the wee hours en-joying last night's festivities, you may be feeling a little under the weather. You could also be the one left to clear away all holiday remnants while others sleep or rest. It will be impossible to please everyone today.

Wednesday the 27th. Take care not to overtax your en-ergies. A big ego might be the cause of current prob-lems. New personal situations can bring more space and freedom. People in authority could be impressed by your personal attributes and qualifications.

Thursday the 28th. The emphasis on career matters con-tinues, with Mercury residing in your solar tenth house of vocation and status. A work project could branch out into a newer area. Now is an excellent time to learn about your limitations and strengths.

Friday the 29th. It may be time to consider trading in your old car for a newer model. Even though you are feeling sociable, you might not want to be surrounded by lots of people this morning. Someone in your inner circle could prove to be unreliable yet again.

Saturday the 30th. A patient and persistent effort is needed. Monitor your spending habits. If you can't af-ford to pay cash for luxury items, wait a little longer un-til you can. You may need to scale down tomorrow night's entertainment because of financial constraints.

Sunday the 31st. A short trip should be fun and may be the start of a new adventure. Not everyone will keep a promise. Minor variations may need to be made to New Year's celebrations. Additional or uninvited guests could put a strain on your resources and wallet.

LIVE PSYCHICS on Your Cell Phone!!!!

Find Your True Love, Romance, Happiness!

Is there money in your future?

Get all of you questions answered NOW!

Your FUTURE could be only a Text Message away!

Text FUTURE to 27777

Text: FUTURE to 27777

From your Cell Phone

.99 - $1.99 per message received 18+

Join The Party, It Never Ends!
See what's happenin' with the GIRLS
And maybe meet some guys TOO!

1-900-288-GIRL

$3.49/min 18+

As seen on CBS's "Crossing Over"

John Edward

One Last Time

*A Psychic Medium Speaks to Those We Have
Loved and Lost*

His television appearances have made millions of
people believe in the afterlife—and in his ability
to reach it.

Now Edward's many fans can read his
remarkable true story and compelling accounts
of his most important readings.

Edward empowers readers to tune in to their own
psychic abilities, to read and understand signs of
spiritual contact they may be
experiencing every day without even knowing it.

**"Compelling...poignant."
—*Publishers Weekly***

0-425-16692-9

**Available wherever books are sold or at
www.penguin.com**

HOROSCOPE DATING

Let the stars help you find the perfect MATCH

CAPRICORN

Dec. 22 to Jan. 19

Characteristics
building, using, organizing, achieving, ordering, climbing

TEXT 'MATCH CAPRICORN'
to number '46898'

AQUARIUS

Jan. 20 to Feb. 18

Characteristics
liberating, knowing, reforming, innovating, researching

TEXT 'MATCH AQUARIUS'
to number '46898'

PISCES

Characteristics
accepting, inspiring, loving, fantasizing, visualizing

Feb. 19 to Mar. 20

TEXT 'MATCH PISCES'
to number '46898'

ARIES

Mar. 21 to Apr. 19

Characteristics
independence, pioneering, fighting, acting, leading

TEXT 'MATCH ARIES'
to number '46898'

TAURUS

Apr. 20 to May. 20

Characteristics
producing, possessing, enjoying, having, maintaining

TEXT 'MATCH TAURUS'
to number '46898'

GEMINI

May 21 to Jun. 21

Characteristics
thinking, communicating, learning, amusing, trading

TEXT 'MATCH GEMINI'
to number '46898'

CANCER

Jun. 22 to Jul. 22

Characteristics
protecting, feeling, dreaming, securing, responding

TEXT 'MATCH CANCER'
to number '46898'

LEO

Jul. 23 to Aug. 22

Characteristics
ruling, respecting, teaching, playing, giving

TEXT 'MATCH LEO'
to number '46898'

VIRGO

Aug. 23 to Sept. 22

Characteristics
improving, working, serving, cleaning, studying

TEXT 'MATCH VIRGO'
to number '46898'

LIBRA

Sept. 23 to Oct. 23

Characteristics
pleasing, socializing, balancing, relating

TEXT 'MATCH LIBRA'
to number '46898'

SCORPIO

Oct. 24 to Nov. 21

Characteristics
concealing, controlling, influencing, transforming, dealing

TEXT 'MATCH SCORPIO'
to number '46898'

SAGITTARIUS

Nov. 22 to Dec. 21

Characteristics
seeking, exploring, travelling, understanding, believing

TEXT 'MATCH SAGITTARIUS'
to number '46898'

HOW HOROSCOPE DATING WORKS
TEXT: MATCH + YOUR SIGN to 46898
and the database using both Western and Chinese astrology
will find and connect you to your best Match.
71% MATCH RESULT GUARANTEED!!!

WHAT DOES YOUR FUTURE HOLD?

DISCOVER IT IN *ASTROANALYSIS*—
**COMPLETELY REVISED THROUGH THE YEAR 2015,
THESE GUIDES INCLUDE COLOR-CODED CHARTS
FOR TOTAL ASTROLOGICAL EVALUATION,
PLANET TABLES AND CUSP CHARTS,
AND STREAMLINED INFORMATION.**

ARIES	0-425-17558-8
TAURUS	0-425-17559-6
GEMINI	0-425-17560-X
CANCER	0-425-17561-8
LEO	0-425-17562-6
VIRGO	0-425-17563-4
LIBRA	0-425-17564-2
SCORPIO	0-425-17565-0
SAGITTARIUS	0-425-17566-9
CAPRICORN	0-425-17567-7
AQUARIUS	0-425-17568-5
PISCES	0-425-17569-3

**Available wherever books are sold or at
www.penguin.com**

Cell Phone Psychics

Horoscopes to Your Cell Phone

Send a text message with your date of birth and get your personalized daily horoscope via text message to your cell phone every day for only $1.99 for a week!

Just Text TOTAL and your birthdate to 82020

If your birthdate is Feb. 15 1968
your message should look like this

TOTAL02.15.68 and be sent to **82020**

Text YOUR Message to a LIVE PSYCHIC

Send a Text message to one of our LIVE Psychics from your cell phone any time, anywhere Just text the word ISEE to 82020 and get the answer to that important question!

Dating - Just Text DATE to 82020

to find that "Special Someone" right on your cell phone!

Chat - Just Text CHAT to 82020

Make new friends, have fun stay connected!

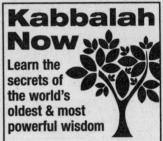